T0271336

I was lucky to have worked with Payal and to know her as an individual. Her sharp intellect, unique understanding of contemporary issues, simple solutions to complex problems and readiness to extend a helping hand endeared her to everyone in her network.

Much later, when I saw her last two books I could not help turning into an admirer. Her worldview and understanding of environments are so different and original. She writes in a simplistic style that is at once friendly and affable. Her earthly logic and illustrative examples are easily understood as they stem from daily life and commonsense. She comes across as an advisor who is effortlessly unpretentious, nonjudgmental and empathetic. I am impressed with her passion to make all her readers succeed in their chosen fields.

It is no wonder that her last book "Achieve Unstoppable Success in Any Economy," was awarded the New York big book award.

I am eagerly awaiting her third book titled "Win the leadership game every time". It is surely going to be as energizing and unputdownable as her previous books.

*Dr. Arun Arora, Chairman, Edvance & Former President,*
*Bennett, Coleman & Company Ltd.*

The first step toward world-class leadership entails learning to lead one's own self. It is a journey of immense courage and magnanimous change. In this book, Payal has integrated the research on leadership development through a multitude of her own coaching experiences across the globe. The result is presented through powerful actionable insights to realize your full potential and also inspire your colleagues and teams for peak performance along the way. Her leadership stories explicitly translate specific behaviors and attributes that can be measured on the pathway to change. Each of these 9 laws will prove to be a valuable guide and springboard for pursuing your hopes, aspirations, dreams, and purpose.

*World Renowned Spiritual Guru Swami Mukundananda, JKYOG*

Playing the game, or playing to win? The exceptional leaders around us share one key common trait—they are not satisfied with good, they always strive for great. They don't just play the game well; they change the game. And in the process, they create movements for impact.

In her book, Payal Nanjiani shares some tried and tested rules of impactful leadership. A much-needed, fresh perspective for all leaders as we lead the way into the new world.

*Paul Dupuis, Chairman and CEO—Randstad Japan,*
*& Author of The E5 Movement*

Payal Nanjiani's new book is both, timely and topical. As we navigate an increasingly ambiguous and uncertain world, the need for leaders in every sphere has never been higher. Further, the framework of leadership itself is changing at an unprecedented pace. Her perspectives on how you win the leadership game in a rapidly evolving ecosystem are refreshingly simple, candid, and laid out in an easy-to-understand and adopt the format. By contextualizing the leadership journey as a game, Payal delivers an authentic take on leadership and how through practice, both existing and new leaders can get more adept at this. This book will be an important and welcome addition to the leadership literature and is a must-read.

*Animesh Kumar, President—HR and Transformation, ZEE*

Congratulations, Payal! Once again, you have a unique and insightful approach to leadership that people from all backgrounds need to hear. Leadership as a game is fascinating and particularly relevant right now—it has changed in a big way over the past few years. The reign of tough, superhero leaders is over, the dawn of vulnerable, sensitive servants is well and truly here. Your constant success is an inspiration to so many others around the world. Thank you for all the opportunities you have extended to me, and I'm excited at what else your future can possibly hold! Here's to even more impact and happiness.

*Josef Werker Co-founder and CEO of Humble Sustainability*
*Managing Director of Penbrother*

Have you ever felt overwhelmed in looking at the gap between where you are in your career and where you want to be? Most good leaders have been there too. One thing you can count on is that in order to win at the game of leadership, you must begin playing the game. Payal Nanjiani has a proven nine laws in her newest book, "Win the leadership game every time," that shows everyone has a path to greatness that is defined within themselves. Join her on a journey to control exactly how you can respond to filling that gap!

*Michelle Proctor, Chief of Staff, Risk Research and*
*Quantitative Solutions Division at SAS*

# Win the Leadership Game Every Time

Payal Nanjiani knows what it takes to win. During her two decades career as a world-renowned executive coach, Payal has helped numerous leaders around the globe succeed at their work and grow through the ranks. Her practices and methods have shown people how to change their thinking, actions and decisions, which helps them win as leaders every time.

*Win the Leadership Game Every Time* is a great read and a great leadership book that offers deep insights, original thinking, and transparent advice that will change the way people think about work. You will read some incredible advice from industry leaders.

Delivering an engaging mix of in-depth business examples and moving personal stories, Payal distills and advances the essentials of winning so you can get maximum effort and peak performance from yourself and your team.

Focusing on the nine laws of winning in leadership and her acclaimed Jugadores Pyramid of Success, this book outlines the mental, emotional, and physical qualities essential to building a winner inside of you.

This book shows you how to develop the confidence and competitive fire to 'be at your best, no matter what.'

# Win the Leadership Game Every Time

## Nine Invaluable Laws to Magnify Your Success

Payal Nanjiani

Routledge
Taylor & Francis Group

A PRODUCTIVITY PRESS BOOK

First published 2023
by Routledge
605 Third Avenue, New York, NY 10158

and by Routledge
4 Park Square, Milton Park, Abingdon, Oxon, OX14 4RN

*Routledge is an imprint of the Taylor & Francis Group, an informa business*

© 2023 Payal Nanjiani

*Library of Congress Cataloging-in-Publication Data*
A catalog record for this title has been requested

ISBN: 978-1-032-19754-8 (hbk)
ISBN: 978-1-032-19699-2 (pbk)
ISBN: 978-1-003-26071-4 (ebk)

DOI: 10.4324/9781003260714

Typeset in Minion
by Newgen Publishing UK

*Dedicated to the winner inside of you.*

Above all, to my husband and dear friend, Ashish Nanjiani—Your love
has always empowered me.

# Contents

# Foreword

Payal has worked with leading corporate leaders and managers across continents, enabling them to perform, deliver, and excel in their professional and personal lives. She is an acknowledged thought leader, guide, and coach who has mastered the art of engaging boards, managers, and front-liners with equal ease and ensuring that she leaves the table with a lot of residual value for the organizations.

An author of two books she now introduces us to the third, and the nine invaluable laws to magnify success. When the book came into my hands, as I turned page after page, I was enthralled as to how she has been able to capture so much insight and convert them into action points for all of us to easily implement. That, I believe, is a hallmark of an author who has engaged very closely with businesses and leaders, learning from them and giving back in multiples.

In these VUCA times this is a much-needed book and it's obvious that with the challenging environment that envelopes all of us, winning as leaders every time and motivating our teams to perform at their highest levels will be a tasking ask and in the midst of this complexity, we need something that is rational, intelligent, and educational to design an approach that will produce the behavior needed for these ambiguous and volatile times. This book easily guides us to the choices we need to make and most importantly the WHY.

As emerging business leaders, academicians, and students, the world we all aspire to build is still being imagined, new frontiers are being challenged every day, and the definition of the road is only based on our beliefs and perceptions, and the possibilities are endless. To enable this task, we will all need to unlock the potential of our teams. I personally believe that every human being is gifted with a huge potential, which can be leveraged to perform at the highest level in every task and situation he/she is.

We can easily convert this gifted human proposition into an equation, **Performance {Potential – Interferences}**, and most of these interferences are self-inflicted, caused by self-beliefs and excuses, may it be personal or even socioeconomical situations, and so on. The author very nicely covered the topic around "Gap Traps" in which many leaders get entangled into and find it difficult to come out of the rut, she points out in each of the nine laws, some of these interferences if first realized, accepted, and worked upon without any inhibition, the concerned leader will surge ahead and avoid getting stuck in self-created cages, entered through the traps. The learning journey must continue and in these few pages what the author has put together is an important ingredient to that.

Having known Payal there was no better person, I would have thought of, to put together the master plan in an easy and lucid manner for all of us to understand. It is a step-by-step guide for winning the game every time without constraints. Winning consistently in an ethical, honest, and sustainable manner matters most, and this book shows the way forward.

The nine invaluable laws have been put forth with very easy examples and this makes the read very enjoyable. If they are imbibed by the reader I assure you that winning will become a habit for you, it will become second nature in your life's journey. The book starts with the Law of Gap and goes on to explain with easy examples on how we can overcome the trap of falling into it.

Clearly, what Payal has put together in this book will improve our way of working, create joy, empower teams, and allow each individual to pursue their goals and dreams. The insights are phenomenally on target.

I thoroughly enjoyed reading this book and I am certain that each one of you will draw valuable lessons from amongst the nine invaluable laws as Payal nudges us to win in the leadership game and achieve success every time.

Enjoy the book.

*Balfour Manuel, Managing Director, Blue Dart*
*Express Limited*

# Acknowledgments

Thanks to the thousands of leaders and entrepreneurs around the world who trusted these laws and have practiced these in their own lives.

To the participants who have attended my keynotes and workshops, I have learned much from you.

To Dr. Arun Arora, CEO of Edvance and a true mentor and friend under whose guidance I have grown and progressed.

To my parents—my mother, Laltoo Malkani, and my father, Ashok Malkani—both of whom gave me unconditional love.

To my husband Ashish and my daughters Ronisha and Rishona for being my constant support.

To my team, for their loyalty and dedication on every project and assignment to ensure that each client gets the best leadership content and service from us.

To Productivity Press for trusting in me and making this book reach its highest potential.

Most importantly, to the higher power, the universe, that guides all hopes and magnifies all good things.

# About the Author

Recognized by the TIMES Group as the most influential personality in the field of leadership speaking and coaching, Payal Nanjiani is an Indian-American leadership expert and executive coach. She is the founder of The Payal Nanjiani Leadership Company, a coaching and training company dedicated to developing transformed leaders who innovate, influence, and implement so that the people, organizations, and the country thrive.

For nearly two decades, Payal's work has been embraced by Fortune 500 companies, top management institutions, celebrity CEOs, entrepreneurs, government officials, and universities.

Her Executive Coaching, Transformative Corporate Leadership Programs, and Power Leadership talks have helped millions of professionals and companies recognize and overcome their leadership challenges and achieve extraordinary levels of success. She is known to get teams to achieve their leadership breakthroughs.

In 2019, she launched The Payal Nanjiani Leadership Podcast to help maximum people in the world become better leaders and overcome their leadership challenges. The podcast, which gained popularity among business leaders, features some of the most prominent leaders, spiritual gurus, and CEOs in the world who share their insights and experience for the global good.

Payal lives with her philosophy Leadership Is Within and believes that "Leadership starts and ends with YOU."

She lives, plays, and works between her home in the North Carolina area of the United States and Bangalore, India.

She can be reached at success@payalnanjiani.com.

Official website: www.payalnanjiani.com

# Introduction: The Rules of the Game

## BE RELENTLESS

Far away in the jungle of Africa, every morning, a deer wakes up and decides to run faster than the fastest cheetah in that jungle. Every morning, a cheetah also wakes up in the same jungle and decides to run faster than the fastest deer that day. Both the deer and the cheetah want to win. The deer wants to win to save its life and the cheetah to satisfy its hunger. They each have their reason to succeed. They are in the game to win. None of them know the end result, yet they decide each day to win.

I often ask my audience two questions during my Unstoppable Leader Workshop, and the two questions are as follows: Are you in the leadership game to win, or are you just playing the game? Do you wake up each morning deciding to win, or do you wake up to go to work simply to get the job done?

My friend, there is a vast difference between working to win and working to just stay in the game. This difference decides where each of us is on the growth ladder and how far we will go. Those playing to be in the game are very concerned about their paycheck and job security. They fear taking risks and are overly cautious. These people view the game as an 'I win you lose' proposition. This group of people works with what I call a weekend mindset, where they wait for the weekend so they can relax and have fun, and they hate Mondays. They work with one leg always on the brake because they're afraid to speed up.

Leaders who play to win and do whatever is necessary to move things forward come from a different level of thinking. They're not reckless but proactive. They make the call that they fear and have that difficult conversation. They deal with the tricky issues that may put their outcomes at risk if things go south on them. These are the people who wake up each

DOI: 10.4324/9781003260714-1

morning with the will to win. They know that winning has nothing to do with power, status quo, position, or playing corporate politics. This set of people isn't intimidated by pressure. They thrive on pressure.

Winning is purely about being relentless and moving ahead in the game by focusing on your improvement and the well-being of others. Winning is about having faith in yourself and your abilities.

Some years back, I was watching the film The Pursuit of Happiness with my family. There was a scene where Chris Gardner, played by Will Smith, announces to his son during a moment of despair:

> Hey. Don't ever let somebody tell you that you can't do something. Not even me. All right? 'You got a dream. You gotta protect it. People can't do something themselves; they want to tell you that you can't do it. If you want something, get it.' Period.

Captured in that brief dialogue is an inspiring reality of what it means to be relentless. To win, you've got to soar above your difficulties persistently. Because if your resolve is firm, nothing can stand in your way to achieving success.

In my years of coaching some athletes, leaders, CEOs, and politicians who are not satisfied with being at the top of their fields, one characteristic sets them apart. They are relentless. They own the ability to never stop trying and pushing toward a goal that only they can see.

To be relentless in the game, you have to be committed to daily actions to pursue your objectives while savoring the journey—for the process is as significant as the goal. You need grit and determination to never give up. You have to promise yourself that you will keep getting back up, no matter how many times you get knocked down. You have to commit yourself to constantly moving forward, no matter what type of adversity comes your way. There will be times when you must change course and alter your plan. This change requires courage. It means you are unwilling to compromise and be comfortable with the situation. It's a state of mind that can give you the courage to be unstoppable and achieve your end result. It means going beyond your job description and craving intensely to deliver more. And the ability to be relentless is in all of us, but only a few play the leadership game relentlessly.

Last year I met two interesting people, Mrs. Harjeet Joshi and Mr. Joe. Their experiences taught me the true meaning of winning the leadership game and how the lack of this attitude can be disastrous to your career.

I had the opportunity of interviewing Mrs. H.K. Joshi on my global podcast—The Payal Nanjiani Leadership Podcast. Mrs. Joshi, Chairperson and Managing Director at the Shipping Corporation of India (SCI), is honored as the only woman Chairperson in the 60 years history of the SCI. During the interview, I asked her if any incidence in her life attributed to her reaching this position. To which she replied with this true-life incidence from her life. During the initial years of her career, she observed that the company wasn't utilizing her talents and abilities to the best. She felt underutilized and frustrated. After three months, she decided to do something that most of us might hesitate to do. She took a paper and pen (yes, those were the days without emails) and wrote a letter to the company's CEO. She introduced herself and what she does at the company and wrote how her talents, skills, and abilities are underutilized. She ended the letter saying that the company was wasting their money by paying her to do what anyone else could do at a much lesser salary. Within a few days, she heard from the CEO, who called her for a quick meeting. He gauged her abilities and worked on critical projects that would leverage her skills and talents. That became a game-changer in her life and got her to move upward in her career. She is what I often teach people to become—a transformed leader.

A transformed leader is someone who has transformed their thinking, action, and behaviors in ways that enable them to consistently perform toward the upper range of their capabilities, regardless of circumstances. They are the ones who have the ability to work hard and have the drive to achieve results, no matter what.

In another incident, at one of my High Impact Leadership trainings, I met Joe, an IT senior manager in a multinational company in the Bay area. After the session, Joe approached me and told me how he was highly frustrated about his situation. He wasn't growing at his job; he felt underutilized and was often passed over for promotions despite his excellent performance. He's been in the same position as an IT senior manager for five years. When I asked him what he was doing about his situation, he grimly said he was desperate to switch jobs and get into a new company.

Both Mrs. Joshi and Joe experienced frustration at their job. Mrs. Joshi was at the entry-level position, with no connections or resources, yet demonstrated the courage to take a bold step and convey her thoughts to the CEO. Joe was at a senior manager level, with resources, credibility, and connections in the organization but was still stuck for five years in his situation without the courage to improve his situation.

Winning doesn't require resources. It requires resourceful thinking.

What creates two different actions in almost similar situations is an individual's thinking pattern. Having coached some of the prominent leaders in the industry, having interviewed the most successful CEOs on my leadership podcast, I've learned well that your thinking can take you uphill or downhill. It's the single most differentiator between the average and exceptional people in the world. And the pandemic situation proved this quite well when some of the countries, organizations and businesses, and leaders managed the situation and came out of it successfully, while others succumbed.

Mrs. Joshi, since her early career days, has been a relentless leader who believes one must never stop in the face of adversity and always dream up creative ways to work around challenging problems. On the other hand, Joe was uncomfortable when faced with adversity. He was always compromising with his situations.

Winning the leadership game means you strive for a level of excellence that very few people are willing to attempt to achieve. It means you have a laser focus on your game and are not vexed about ruining another's game or running someone else's game. True relentless leaders aren't satisfied with being good or even great; they want to be unstoppable.

---

## FEED THAT ADDICTION

My first real awareness that leadership is a serious business game came when I met coach Felipe at the football stadium in Chile, South America. My good friend and business associate, Alexis, who owned a car tire shop, sponsored the Chile team to play the all-women football tournament in Peru, and Coach Felipe from Chile was in charge of women's football in Chile. During my three days' stays in Chile, I had the opportunity to visit the stadium with Alexis. It is here that I got to know the tragic story of coach Felipe. Felipe was an impeccable football player and had represented Chile in many international tournaments. In 2001, during one of the tournaments in Chile, he was fouled, and the match cost the sponsor their reputation and money. Later media outlets circulated a photograph of Coach Filipe shaking hands with the Peru team captain. The sporting gesture was misunderstood, and Felipe was suspected of 'throwing' the game out of some 'take' from Peru. For 11 years, Filipe carried this humiliation and felt his life buried under it. When in the year 2012 he got an offer from Alexis to coach an all-women football team, Felipe readily took it up. He worked tirelessly, crossed all challenges, and did whatever it would take to get this team to win the tournament and, eventually, the team won a gold medal. That day I witnessed closely the moment when you wipe the chlorinated water from your eyes, and you overpower any number of giant squids along the way. Coach Felipe earned his respect back. I realized how leadership is a game everyone wants to win.

What makes the leadership game interesting is that there are different players in the game, and all players are playing at different levels. What is needed is the will to win. You must be a relentless player. Felipe was relentless to win even after 12 years of that humiliation. And it is often seen that a relentless outlook can make those around you uncomfortable, and they soon begin to impose their shortcomings on you to appease their indignity.

Here's a leader's greatest truth: Leaders who wake up to win are highly self-directed and able to absorb the inevitable criticism, obstacles, challenges, and setbacks. They keep their eyes on completing the mission and find creative solutions when things don't go as planned. They are relentless in the leadership game. And the bigger your game, the harder it is to win, the more relentless you will need to be in your thinking, attitude, and actions.

Being relentless is a state of mind that can give you the strength to achieve, survive, overcome, and be strong when others are not. The ability to be relentless is in all of us. It is this attitude that gets you your unstoppable wins. Relentless leaders can absorb the inevitable criticism, obstacles, challenges, and setbacks and keep advancing. They keep their eyes on completing the mission and are willing to find creative solutions when things don't go as planned.

And winning is an addiction that you must feed. Once you taste victory, you want more and more of it. This craving for more is what you want to provide inside of you. Keeping your integrity and values, you must feed the winning addiction. Let the fear of losing be big inside of you. O.J. Simpson, an American football player, said, 'fear of losing makes competitors so great. Show me a gracious loser, and I'll show you a permanent loser.' A failure is never an option, I agree.

Many years back, the vice president of the company where I was working as an HR head asked me a question that left a lasting impression on me and later became the source of origination of my coaching work. He asked me, 'Are we a world-class team?' At that moment, I felt that indeed we are a world-class team that uses the latest cutting-edge technologies, have the best engineers, and constantly meet our targets.

However, I was like a frog in the well who thought the world was the well in which it lives. All companies concentrate on their training and numbers. All teams are encouraged to deliver the best and get the numbers. They set goals, plan, attend meetings, and work long hours. Then what sets apart one from another? As I got more curious with this question playing in my mind at all times, I realized that the world-class teams are the ones who perform with the idea of winning meaningfully. A winner stays committed to winning, no matter what. How do you do that?

You train your brain to win. You train it to win against self-doubt and negativity and to make meaningful wins. You carve a path of your own. You condition yourself to find excellence in solitude. Winning is an addiction, and you stay addicted by consistently working on yourself. Winners never let the addiction control them. Instead, they remain in control by deciding to pull back, refocus, and return with a renewed appetite for more.

To be the best in your field of work, it's never satisfying to just get to the top; you've got to stay there, and then you've got to climb higher because, otherwise, you will begin to settle.

If every person in the workforce has this type of authentic winning addiction, whatever be the definition of the win for them, can you imagine what our workforce would look like? The results would be miraculous, for one and all.

## ACCEPT THE BRUTAL TRUTH NO ONE TELLS YOU

Since my early days at work, I remember being very fascinated by the word leadership. And when you are fascinated by something, you want to know more about that subject; you are curious to learn more. So, I delved deep into books. One book said to be a great leader; you must set a goal; the other said it's all about time management and so on. And I kept reading about leadership, and soon, my knowledge about this subject increased.

Then one day, there was a leadership position open in the company I worked for in those days. I was super excited to apply for it. After all, I had read so many books on leadership. However, I wasn't considered for the role. I was broken and discouraged when they chose another colleague over me, even though we had similar work experience and skills. For the next few months, I felt depressed and believed that organization did not value me. I began searching for another job, thinking it would solve my problem and stand a better chance to get into a leadership position. How wrong I was. Today people come to me from all over the world asking me to coach them to become what I call—world-class transformed leaders. If only I knew then what I know now after coaching many super successful leaders and celebrity CEOs. If only at that time someone would have held my hand and whispered to me the brutal truth about leadership—that leadership has nothing to do with your title, role, designation, country, position, status, or your job description. If I only knew that I am a leader, no matter what. And what I am going to tell you now is what I tell people who want to win the leadership game. That leadership is all about willingness.

Be willing to do the extra work. You can't have a 9-5 mindset and go paycheck to paycheck expecting to be successful. You've got to be willing to put in that extra work; the extra work to get better at what you do—the extra work to be a master in your field. You've got to be willing to be lonely on your way to leadership because you've got to be committed to giving it your everything, and people around you will not understand that. They may not understand that vision that the universe has given to them. So, they will begin to pull away from you, or maybe you might have to decide to pull away from them. Be willing to walk alone and keep cheerleading until you get there. Winning the leadership game is about being willing to change your behavior and adapt to your environment. It's about being ready to lead in the toughest of situations. Winning means being hungry for more knowledge, more growth, and more success. You can't be sitting there satisfied with your life, feeling content with what you have.

No one told me that winning the leadership game means you've got to be willing to overcome that negative talk and self-doubt and that you must stand up and sell yourself every day on your abilities. Those rejections and failures will be crowned on you, and you've still got to be willing to smile and move ahead.

People, society, and business magazines failed to point out that I must be willing to practice and master my craft. And that mastering my craft will require a lot of patience, commitment, and consistency. To be a master in my field, I will need to begin my day before anyone else and keep working after everyone else has stopped.

No one told me all of this. But I am telling you this because I want you to win the leadership game. I want you to grow and succeed at what you do. I want you to lead a remarkable work life, and I genuinely want you to step into your greatness. And so, I want to tell you upfront—winning the leadership game is about willingness. It's not about who you are; it's not about your title, job description, or team. It's not about power or about playing corporate politics. It's about being willing.

What are you willing to do to be a winner? Are you willing to read, learn? Are you willing to listen? Are you willing to be self-aware, accept feedback and criticism, and put that feedback into play? Are you willing to be humble and to recognize you are not the only person in your world? Are you willing to influence others positively, without any benefit to yourself? The question here is as follows: Are you genuinely willing to do the work to get to the next level? Are you willing to win? Are you willing to do whatever it takes? What sacrifices are you willing to make? What trade-offs are you willing to make? Are you willing to fail again and again and again?

Most people are not living their dreams. A lot of people never do things they want to do. Most people live an average life, going paycheck to paycheck. They've stopped believing that they are meant to lead an extraordinary life. They settle for whatever they get. They doubt themselves. They let others decide their path. They work in a survival mode and fear rejections and failures. And soon, career life comes to an end. And you wonder what you ever do with the time and opportunities you had here? You were here to create an impact, to do something extraordinary, and to fulfill your dreams. But sadly, many of us leave our professional lives feeling unfulfilled and regretful. We have goals, dreams, and visions. But we play the game not expecting to win. Honestly, we don't really believe we can attain our goals. We may, deep down, think of ourselves as unlucky, as losers, as not being good enough to achieve the goals we have set and win. How can you win with this attitude?

The times we are in are testing our willingness to win. Leaders who make it will do what it takes to win while keeping their values and integrity.

## LEADERSHIP THROUGH MIND

There are almost 7.5 billion people on the planet Earth. Out of these, if we are to focus on those in the workforce, we can roughly say there are

3.5 billion in the workforce, as per the United Nations Department of Economic and Social Affairs. Now, you and I both know the tiny percentage of highly successful people in their careers who are high achievers and deliver outstanding results compared to the many stuck at the bottom or mid-level in the ladder. And guess what. These people who are stuck in their career are actually working extremely hard. Yet the needle doesn't move significantly for them.

While visiting companies to coach their executives and conduct leadership trainings for their teams, I see how the people in an organization perform. Here is a pyramid explaining how people in an organization are distributed. I call it the *Jugadores* pyramid. Jugadores is a Spanish word for players. Every organization has these Jugadores who play at different levels.

As you can see in Figure 0.1, the pyramid has three types of Jugadores or players in the corporate world—the passive Jugadores, the active Jugadores, and the transformed Jugadores.

The passive players can be found at the bottom of the pyramid, which consists of the 15% of people who are the underperformers and nonproducers. They are only concerned with keeping their paycheck, and at first sight of a problem, they would leave the ship and run. They have no desire to grow upward in the organization or in their life. Passive players

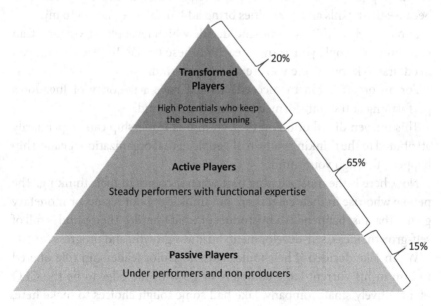

**FIGURE 0.1**
15%, 65%, and 20%—The Jugadores Pyramid.

are performers who are not achieving enough to satisfy their employers and are most likely to be asked to move along.

The active players are in the mid-level of the pyramid, which consists of the 65% of people who are the backbone of any organization; these are the group who are well trained and mentored on various skill sets. They work extra hard and work dedicatedly. They follow instructions and give instructions downward. Some are keen to get into higher positions and grow. Many on this level of the pyramid have reached the mid-level on the corporate ladder, and the journey ahead is something that becomes challenging for many. This level of players has functional expertise. They are competent, steady performers who balance their work and personal lives while still doing the bulk of the company's work. Active players tend to stay put, don't require a lot of attention, and get the job done.

The transformed players from the top of the pyramid consist of 20% of highly self-directed people. They develop goals, strategic plans, company policies, and make decisions on the direction of the business. They achieve one goal after another; the company depends on them for ideas and growth; they are super achievers and high-income earners. Transformed players are the risk-takers, the 'high potentials,' and employers enjoy finding and hiring them. They are the players who keep your business running. They are the top performers whom employers prioritize due to their resources because their skills and specialties bring added value to the company.

Look closely at this pyramid and decide which level player you are. Can you think of people you know at each of these levels? To play to win, you need first to know where you are on this pyramid.

For an organization to succeed, it must have a majority of Jugadores performing at the transformed level on the pyramid.

This uneven distribution on the pyramid of leadership can be primarily attributed to the thinking pattern of people in that organization. Leadership happens through your mind.

Now, here is the most exciting part when it comes to their thinking. The people who rise in their careers are not thinking about results or monetary gains. That just happens as a byproduct of what they do. Their mind is full of self-growth, ideas, self-development, business growth, and progress for all.

When Jake decided if he should take the senior leadership role offered to him in his current large company or go with the offer to be the CEO of a relatively small company, Jake had some tough choices to make here. If he stuck around his current company, his income would be more than he was currently making. His position would be of a higher status quo, and his comfort zone of knowing the company and its operation would remain. But somehow, all of this did not excite him. He was aware that the new company that offered the CEO role was small in terms of annual sales and employees and that his income wouldn't equal what his current company was offering him. But here's what Jake was thinking. He believed he had untapped potential and could help the company double its sales and profits. Jake was aware of his excellent leadership skills. He already began thinking of ways the company could come out of its current situation and grow. He decided to take the CEO's offer even though he had never led an organization. His thinking got him to make the choice most of us would not have. He did not think about money or safety net but rather how he could apply his expertise to help the company progress.

Successful people think differently as compared to average people. They create a mindset that leads them toward success in life. Most people remain average because they never think about their thinking. As it's said, 'you become what you think about.'

Now, if you know me well, you know I am curious and always love to ask questions. While at a dinner with a CEO of a mid-size company, I asked him the secret of his outrageous success at such a young age of 42 years. He smiled and replied, 'I make time to think.' I looked at him, wondering just how making time to think can get someone to be so successful. Well, my doubt did not last long as he continued saying,

> Payal, every morning, I spend at least 45 minutes with my eyes closed, deep in reflection, just thinking. Sometimes I analyze business challenges. Other times I am thinking about new markets. At other times, I reflect on the meaning of my life and what I want it to stand for. Often, I am simply dreaming up new ways to grow. Payal, I've done this right from the beginning of my career. I want my thinking to be big and long.

I was in awe of what he said. My stomach was already full with his words, and I had no desire to eat the lavish dinner on my plate. On my way home, I constantly asked myself why I did not spend time like him in deep thinking? It isn't such a complex or demanding task. Often the simple tasks are the hardest to start, I feel. But I started. The very next day, I started to consciously dedicate some time in the day, each day, to think. Initially, it was hard. But gradually, within two weeks, it became simple. I began thinking of everything—from new ideas to building new connections, reflecting upon the learnings, new ways to add value to the lives of my clients, and so much more. It helped me succeed and provided people and organizations the value I wanted to.

What about you? How much time do you dedicate daily to think?

People who are winners in the leadership game are great thinkers. They evaluate their leadership game through their mind. If you have read my book Achieve Unstoppable Success in Any Economy, you might remember the priming technique I wrote about. Priming gets you to change your state of mind to achieve your desired results. The origin of leadership is your mind, just where doubt origins too.

Have you observed how some individuals become frustrated by the demands and pressures of leadership, while others say they are not cut out to be leaders? Many people tend to model the leadership traits of leaders they admire or have encountered, hoping that replicating the behaviors of leaders they perceive to be successful will make them successful. Rarely does this type of approach to leadership work. There is something so basic to successful leadership that it is often missed. It is the mind—and how it works is the key to being a successful leader. Mastery of the mind is required to become a leader.

When we take on the task of leadership, we must first recognize where our ability to lead resides. It is not in what we do that is seen by others. It is what is going on inside our minds that produce our ability to lead. To be effective, we must focus on the internal dynamics of our minds to know who we are as leaders.

Your mind is where positive and negative thoughts, which shape your present and future leadership behaviors, are formed. Your success as a leader begins in your mind, and the ability to be a successful leader depends on how you utilize your mind. Being relentless in the leadership game begins in mind. Being willing to be a transformed player begins in mind. Winning begins in mind.

## RACE AGAINST TIME

Everyone is in a race against time. Every leader, every CEO, every entrepreneur, and every person in the workforce today is in a race against time.

Francis Crick, who won a Nobel Prize for co-discovering the DNA double helix, worked from his hospital bed even when he died of cancer. Similarly, Isaac Asimov, who had written over 450 books, was asked, 'What would you do if you had six months to live?' He replied, 'Type faster.'

We're all in the ultimate race against time. We're chasing something. There are so many things we want to achieve. We want to fulfill those dreams; we want to buy that big house; we want to get to that position we so desire; we want to prove ourselves. We squeeze all our desires and wants into our work lives while we are able. It's a self-created race that we get into by reading about the rich and famous people. Our work culture teaches us that being busy is best. And this is obvious in the way we're running and taking up more work than ever. Many of us are overbooked and running on a low tank or, in some cases, running on empty—and racing against the clock simultaneously.

They say career life is like a rat race. You want to get to your destination as fast as possible. You want to go ahead of others.

However, I feel it is a unique race; it's a race against time; not everyone can run for a long time, some have many years left, and some may have few minutes, but the point is to run as fast as you can before your time runs out. In the end, it's only a race if we are competing with ourselves. Winning the leadership game is about who will cross the finish line, not who will cross it first.

As a leader, we are encouraged to vision the future. You, I, and most of us might have so many ideas that we want to fulfill, and we want to move faster with all of those ideas. We want to do them now.

At one of the business management universities in India, where I was invited to speak about developing unshakable confidence, most students had this question, 'how can I be successful fast?' The stress was on the word *fast*. We want to fulfill those dreams now. We want to win now. We want to sow the seed and reap the harvest in the same season. We are in a hurry. But I want you to know this—winning takes time. Winning is a process, and it's slow. Most people have a strong desire to win. But because they want it quick, it makes them impatient, shortcut-minded, and capricious, all of which have devastating effects on performance. Overnight success does not exist. You can't have it all in a short period.

I once learned from a very sage business tycoon that one must never keep their ideas in their mind. You must write them down. And then you work toward them but never get overwhelmed by them, and don't rush into fulfilling them. Work diligently and work hard to complete your dream, one goal at a time, one day at a time. And always remind yourself that what is meant for you will find its way to you. The universe will never pass by you and will not forget to get to you what is meant for you. The universe is in no rush and is not in a race against time. We humans are.

Make it your daily mantra to *run until you cross the finish line*. Because in the end, we are all answerable to ourselves.

The scripture reads, 'In a race, everyone runs, but only one person gets first prize. So run your race to win.' What this means is that you are not in a competition with anyone. Not even with time. Befriend time, do what it does. It moves ahead, and so must you.

Too many of us also grew up believing that winning requires sacrifice, grim determination, and intense ambition. As a result, we may have struggled for years and even reached some of our goals but wound up feeling exhausted, our lives out of balance. Undoubtedly, throughout our work life, we inevitably have to deal with work pressure, an unpleasant boss, failures, deadlines, and many unpleasant and challenging situations and people. All of this plays on our emotions, and we blame these situations and people for our slow growth and failures. When we face difficult people and problems, they play on our emotions, and we deal with them in ways that are detrimental to our growth. We fall into self-destructive patterns of thinking and behaving, and that's when despite our efforts, knowledge, experience, and expertise, we lose the game at which we are masters. And this is what makes winning impossible for many.

Winning is about making choices. When you choose one option, you are also saying no to many other choices. You can have what you want, but you cannot want it all and have it all. My father always reminded me that to go to the East, you will have to leave the West and vice versa. I find it incredible when I meet people who have been bouncing from one job to another, from one online network club to another, thinking they will soon see the right trick to 'hack' success. Winning is hidden deep beneath strategy, sacrifices, and hard work. And most of all, it requires you to work on yourself.

My younger daughter had developed an interest in chess at the young age of seven years. As she was learning the game from the chess instructor, I observed that the game on its own isn't very tough. The main reason why we lose at chess is that we make unnecessary mistakes. The big question is, how can we eliminate these mistakes from our game, or at least keep them to an absolute minimum? The instructor taught my daughter to look back at critical moments within games where errors are made and examine how we can recognize the danger signs and avoid making impulsive decisions.

Most of us don't analyze our game and so someone around us will be more than happy to leverage our weakness and demonstrate what we've done wrong. At every level, you have to play the game better to win. The only way to better the game and increase your winning chances is to better yourself. The nine laws in this book are to help you do exactly just that. It enables you to change your strategy to experience a more satisfying work life without racing against time.

## WHEN YOU LOSE, IT HURTS REALLY BAD

Have you ever felt like you weren't allowed to fail? Or have you ever lost at something you wanted to win? And what happens when you mess up? Do you feel hopeless, frustrated, and say to yourself, 'I'm tired of losing? Winning is not for me.' Guess what? It's hard to win when you're feeling down and when you lose faith in your ability to win. If you really want to win the leadership game every time, you've got to know how to turn your failures into your wins every time.

I know when you're losing, everything hurts. And it hurts really bad. And then with time, you begin to overcome that hurt but then it shows up at the wrong place again and again. Just when you have to give that important presentation, your mind like a faithful servant will bring back memories of the failure you had seven months back while presenting. And the hurt, the wound becomes fresh again in your mind, paralyzing you and then you lose your current presentation too. And that's how your mind traps you into the cycle of imposter syndrome, self-doubt, and the 'I can't do it' type of thoughts.

I've experienced many wins in my life. But I've had more than my share of losses. Failures and losses cause us to get emotionally stuck. We feel mentally defeated. We lose our spirit in the face of failures. Guess what? I've failed on an epic scale—an exceptionally short-lived success at my first job. Jobless during the first few years in America, I failed at my early career stint in corporate America. At that time, by every usual standard, I was the biggest failure I knew.

Now I look around and see a team of amazing people around me. This is so powerful because for so long, I was in this alone. Nobody understood my vision. Oh, and I couldn't even explain or clearly define it. I think back to start my journey as an entrepreneur and my first office was in my home garage.

I had refused to roll over and die. I learned how to flip failures to wins. During the years of career confusion and being frustrated with outgrowing every job, I began to see around me millions of people in the workforce who were stuck in their careers despite all their hard work. Those people wanted to win but did not know how to win. They did not even know how to play the game. But I knew—both the game and how to play to win. I knew what it takes to reach high up. In my conversations with some of the most successful leaders, I learned how they had played the game. And I decided to help people become transformed leaders and win the game.

And since then, my life has changed for the better. I worked in Corporate America and held many leadership roles. I later started my own training and coaching company to help leaders recognize and overcome their leadership challenges and become transformed leaders who influence, inspire, and implement with speed and serenity.

Being an executive coach, I've observed there are two ways of winning the game. One, by playing dirty corporate politics, bumping others to reach your goal, thinking solely about your growth, working in a state of frustration, and being selfish. This way, maybe you win, but you lose your peace of mind and ultimately health. And this type of win soon becomes meaningless.

Another better way to win is by transforming yourself, so you improve in the game each day. These nine laws will help you do just that. And the results are miraculous. When you begin to apply each of these laws in your own life, you will develop clarity about your work life, have unshakable confidence in yourself, and know how to profit from failure. It is to help you to become a transformed leader who is highly self-directed and can strategically deal with people and situations. It will be a meaningful win and will stay with you forever because it is said that the only conquests that are permanent and leave no regrets are our conquests over ourselves. And when you are no longer afraid of the hurt or failure and have started breathing life into the success within you, you truly win.

## PLAY TO WIN THE ULTIMATE GAMBLE ON YOURSELF

I've seen many employees trying to rise higher in their careers, but, unfortunately, most of them fail. What causes people to fail? What gets their career growth to slow down? It happens because they do their jobs just as much as needed, while secretly hoping that they will get promoted one day. It rarely works like this.

After many years of watching the winners in the corporate world, I've had one interesting observation that it's clear to me that putting the exclusive focus on climbing up the career ladder leads to failure. When a person's eyes are on the ultimate result only (to be at the 'highest point' in their career or get that next position or crack the numbers), they tend to neglect important things like personal growth, skills development, and cooperation with other people. Not only do they ignore these things, but they fail to realize that these things are essentials for rising high and attaining recognition. Conventional wisdom suggests that the way to success is to stay in your lane, work hard while climbing the corporate ladder—one position at a time and building relations with people within your industry. But research suggests that this path is far less valuable. So, what works?

There are specific laws of growth and success. To win the game of leadership, you must be aware of these laws and practice them daily. Let me explain.

Have you ever played the lottery or poker? What about video games or any sport? While playing any game, you start with conditioning yourself to win. You enter the game to win. You want to win. And you begin to make your choices—on the number to bet on, on the person to kill in the video game. You bet and hope the results are in your favor.

Winning the leadership game is like playing any sport or virtual game. You make a bet. Every day, moment by moment, we make choices. Every day we make decisions, and each decision, whether big or small, forces us to bet either on ourselves or against ourselves. When you bet, you're taking a chance. You believe in what's right about you. You believe in your potential. You believe in your dreams. And our beliefs rarely disappoint us.

When Sudha left her job to take care of the house and children, she was happy with her family life. Soon as the kids grew and were independent, she was bored with her life. She went into depression, was sick with anxiety, panic attacks, and stomach ulcers. She slept for long hours. She was tired of the housework and was more than often taken for granted by her husband. One day she heard me talk at a women's day event attended by more than 1500 women globally. She reached out to my office and signed up for her 1:1 coaching. Throughout the session, she realized that she had stopped believing in herself. Her husband often told her she was good for nothing; these words from him were destroying her internally. She was alive and breathing despair each day. She thought that she was dependent on her husband's approval from everything. Somewhere she had left that bold and courageous Sudha behind. She felt like a loser. I worked with her in every session to get her to where she wanted to be in her career. Today, Sudha is the owner of a financial company and empowers many young women to win in their lives.

Charles wanted to play it big in the retail market. He was happy with his job, but his deep desire was to be an entrepreneur. He had a great idea to create an app for the retail industry that would connect all company owners and allow them to network closely in their industry.

What stopped him from playing big? His doubts and fear. He was too afraid to trust his abilities and his power to win. He retired from his office at the age of 58 and to date regrets not having lived the life he wanted to.

Both Sudha and Charles were afraid to bet on themselves to win. We don't bet on ourselves because we don't trust ourselves. We don't trust the universe that created us to be unique. We don't have confidence in the higher power who trusted us and sent us on this planet Earth for fulfilling a great purpose. You won the race for life from among more than a million sperms, and you were born. Your race started even before life. You won before you were born. And the fact you are here today means you are still alive to win.

There are ways too many unbelievably talented people settling for a job, because they are too scared to bet on themselves. The fastest way to win is to bet on yourself. Period!

Las Vegas is a favorite holiday destination for my husband and me. Here I see people willing to drop hundreds of thousands of dollars by gambling on their favorite number or card but not reinvest that same amount on themselves.

Gambling on yourself isn't easy. It requires thick skin and adaptability, understanding that no day is the exact same.

I wouldn't say I like to gamble, but if there's one thing I am willing to bet on is myself. And I've always done it. I've bet on myself and still do. Because if you don't bet high on yourself, no one else ever will. When the stakes are high and you are unsure who's got your back, you have to bet on yourself to win. You've known YOU your entire life. You know your strengths and weaknesses, your likes and dislikes, and what you're passionate about.

Betting on yourself is the quickest way to success. Waiting for the world to permit you to win is the way to mediocrity. Remember these are the times when the longer you stay with a company, the less valuable you are.

And ultimately, winning or losing in the game of leadership is not in your control.

Finally, luck plays its part: chance, a word regularly debated between my father and me. I am often intrigued by just how much of this variance is often left *unexplained*. My father would often say that a person can do their best, but ultimately luck becomes a deciding factor. He would often give me the example of throwing a ball in the air. You might be the perfect server and catcher, but when the ball is tossed into the air, you don't know whether a sudden gust of wind will force it to change its momentum or direction, which might get you to miss that catch, making it a perfect trap for your competitor who did not expect it. So, the only thing you can do is focus on your game. Because ultimately, you must play the game. And you must play it to win.

Bet on yourself because you deserve it. Be the maker of your fate. Who else do you trust more than yourself? All of the super successful people I know of living their dream life because they decided to bet on themselves.

---

## THE NEW NATURE OF BUSINESS

The rules of business are changing. The game is evolving with speed. New markets are emerging. A new generation of workforce is entering the game. One can't play the new leadership game with old rules and competencies. Working with some great leaders has shown me how a leader can move with agility, speed, and flexibility to revamp the organization when faced with a business crisis. A leader's decisive and bold actions and their rapid and insightful response to crisis demonstrated the value of speed and serenity in setting a new course for their company.

What are the new rules and competencies? How do we play and win the leadership game every time? Many people playing the leadership game from the middle of the pyramid believe that their skill, talent, and hard work will get them to the top. And this thinking gets them more than often stuck where they are. It takes them years to move ahead in the direction they wish to. They become like a rat in the wheel, moving but getting nowhere.

As work and organizations have become more fluid, strategy is no longer about planning years ahead. Still, about sensing and seizing new opportunities and adapting to a constantly changing environment, you require a new and a different playbook that helps you win your game.

This book is filled with examples of forward-thinking leaders who have adopted radical new opportunities to win the leadership game. Their winning has contributed to the winning of their teams and organization.

Here are a few questions to ask yourself and clarify, so you know how to play and win.

1. What does winning the leadership game mean for you?
2. Where will you play?
3. Do you have a winning strategy?
4. In what areas do you want to win?
5. Why do you want to win?
6. How are you going to play the moves?
7. How do you improve in the game?
8. What do you need to do to stay in the game and move ahead?

I believe leadership is a serious business game we all must play in our career life. It's an easy game, not simple, though. It has its complexities and challenges. Yet each of us must play the game with dedication, consistency, and purposefully. Don't give up the game just because someone is ahead of you in the game or because you had a late start, or because things didn't go your way. It's ok to slow down in the game for a little while before you pick up again. But don't stop because of power play, favoritism, nepotism, or corporate politics. These are challenges of the game, which you must cross.

Imagine if every single day you woke up to win the leadership game. Then at the end of each day, you find yourself full of energy, newly inspired to deliver more, and freshly committed to what brought you into the corporate world in the first place. Wouldn't it be a fantastic feeling to be a part of something larger than yourself, to make a difference, and to live a purposeful life while earning a great living?

I have a great desire to help people win in their games. I got into coaching and speaking to help people succeed in their work lives. So as you start into this book, understand that the person most desirous of you to win is me, your friend and mentor Payal Nanjiani. It's why I've taken the time to write this book. I believe that the universe has blessed me with the opportunity to associate with some of the top leaders across varied industries, not to walk away with so much learning that would benefit only me. I have constantly transferred to people my knowledge, experience, and practices that I learn from these players to know the insiders' secrets of winning. And you can win when you apply these laws to your everyday life.

Because ultimately, winning is an inside job.

## GET OUT OF THE PACK

No one knew it was coming. No astrologer, no finance expert, no company, no country predicted or warned the world of the massive global economic crisis 2020 would bring. Suddenly, the share market crashed, people began losing jobs overnight, and company executives were told to conserve the company's cash in case the financial contagion spread. The production rate at every company was slowing; sales were collapsing, many businesses were forced to shut down their warehouses and vertices. As I wrote this book amid this pandemic, most of the leaders I talked with were either deeply worried or scared. Every executive I met asked me two critical questions—how bad is it now? How bad could it get? The answers were grim. A pandemic hit the world—yes, a real pandemic, the coronavirus disease 2019 (Covid-19) that swept the world by panic as people began to lose confidence in themselves, in their company, and everything around them.

I knew the world had faced a business crisis earlier, like 9/11 or the Great Recession, and the world will continue to face many more worst problems. But let me be honest here. No one has ever seen such a vortex before. Some experts said it would take a year for the global economy to revive; others said it would take up to five. However, I also found leaders who had begun to re-shape their business and themselves to carry on through whatever hard time lay ahead. They are making rapid and new changes, preparing for growth, and preparing to enter new markets. Some are moving faster toward grabbing opportunities and serving customers in different ways. These are the people who will emerge as game-changers.

What differentiated these few companies from the majority? Why do some people emerge as game-changers and win amid any crisis? I got the answer to this question when my daughter told me she feels she has #FOMO. I had never heard of this word before and asked her what that meant. She stared at me as if I asked one of the dumbest of all questions. She said, 'Mom, seriously, don't you know FOMO means "fear of missing out," like a feeling or perception that everyone else is leading a better life, experiencing better things, and having more fun than you are.' Oh, I get it; it could affect your self-esteem and trigger a deep sense of envy. Many of us feel the same FOMO at our work too. We think others are taking up a course, so we should too. If others are playing politics, we should too; if everyone is working extra hours, we should too, and if all are saying bad things about a boss, they are correct; we too should say these things about them. However, if we give importance to doing what others are doing, when will we do anything different from what we were created? Many of us think that being different from the norm reflects poorly on us. We tend to look differently at people whose actions, behavior, or looks do not conform to our idea of normal. Contrary to this belief, the ingenious Albert Einstein once said, 'The person who follows the crowd will usually go no further than the crowd. The person who walks alone is likely to find himself in places no one has ever seen before.' and his words hold to this day.

If you look closely at people who have achieved massive success, you will notice that they are not like everyone else. They achieved success because they dared to be different. They realized that following the crowd mindlessly kills creativity and limits capabilities, thereby ultimately preventing them from attaining the greatness they were meant for. Winning, by its very definition, is a deviation from the norm. The norm is an average or a standard level. It's where the majority of people wind up. You are not meant to be in the majority if you are reading this book.

If you want to win the leadership game, you must get out of the pile—the pile of mediocrity, the pile of fear, the pile of averageness.

As I talk to you about getting out of the pack, I am reminded of a beautiful story I once read.

*There was this museum laid with beautiful marble tiles, with a huge marble statue displayed in the middle of the lobby. Many people came from all over the world just to admire this beautiful marble statue.*

*One night, the marble tiles started talking to the marble statue.*

*Marble tile: 'Marble statue, it's just not fair, it's just not fair! Why does everybody from all over the world come all the way here just to step on me while admiring you? Not fair!'*

*Marble statue: 'My dear friend, marble tile. Do you still remember that we were actually from the same cave?'*

*Marble tile: 'Yeah! That's why I feel it is even more unfair. We were born from the same cave, and yet we receive different treatment now. Not fair!'*

*Marble statue: 'Do you still remember the day when the designer tried to work on you, but you resisted the tools?'*

*Marble tile: 'Yes, of course, I remember. I hate that guy! How could he use those tools on me! It hurt so badly!'*

*Marble statue: 'That's right! He couldn't work on you at all as you resisted being worked on.'*

*Marble tile: 'So???'*

*Marble statue: 'When he decided to give up on you and start working on me instead, I knew at once that I would be something different after his efforts. I did not resist his tools. Instead, I bore all the painful tools he used on me.'*

*Marble statue: 'My friend, there is a price to everything in life. Since you decided to give up halfway, you can't blame anybody who steps on you now.'*

Here's my message to you. To succeed and to be the best, you've got to be like the marble statue. The harder the knocks you go through in life, the more you learn and put them to use in the future. Rather than feeling like a victim, think of the result and be a winner. You have to find the edge. And then push past it.

When hit by any business or economic crisis, the immediate challenge is to act quickly and decisively to prepare for the worst possible scenario. This means many leaders will have to bring about a huge change, a massive transformation in themselves. The question is, how many are ready to bring about this transformation in themselves? This readiness to transform is not simple. It takes effort, discipline, and consistency, which is why we see few win the leadership game every time.

Succeeding in a volatile environment requires stability and frequent adjustments. This means as a leader, you are highly self-directed and know how to manage your inner leader, a concept you might have read in my earlier two books—Success Is Within and Achieve Unstoppable Success in Any Economy.

It's not enough today to sit in your office, take up more work, and issue or follow instructions. You need a thorough understanding of what is happening inside and outside your company. You need to think big and long. You have to be involved, visible, and in the execution mode.

---

## PLAYING THE WRONG GAME

For you to emerge as a game-changer, you must know how to win the leadership game. The problem is most of us are playing the wrong game. I know of numerous people who work tirelessly to position themselves for a promotion. They took a job they were more than qualified for because they believed in the company, took the projects no one else wanted, knocked them out of the park, and even mentored new teammates until they became self-sufficient stars. They joined and supported the company's internal groups to be more visible. But despite their hard work, most of the time, the promotion would be given to someone else. Another person gained visibility. In this book, I have explained why this happens and how to overcome this obstacle. The problem is many don't realize that the game has changed. Some of the signs the game has changed are that you face the same problem repeatedly, grow slow at your work, achieve your goals, become more arduous, and get tired in your pursuit to win.

How many people tell me that when a problem arises, they will play to win when a deep crisis grips them. More than often, during tough times, people lose the game simply because they haven't been playing to win every single day, in all the small instances of daily work life. They lose the game, both from the inside and outside. Most people play the game just to be in the game.

A couple of years back, I met Kevin at one of the sandwich shops in San Francisco. At the billing counter, Kevin greeted me in a very routine manner and put my order on the computer, and asked me to swipe my card, which I did. Then on my way out, I realized I had been billed for a soda bottle that I hadn't ordered. I went back to Kevin, who looked at the bill and then looked up at me and said rudely, 'you should have been careful while swiping your card.' He then did the process of billing once again. I thought to myself of how he handled a minor situation like this one offensively, blaming the customer. He indeed was just in the game for his paycheck.

While coaching a boxing champion, I learned that daily practice and grinding develop your ability to win any game. You must immerse yourself in complexity repeatedly to be prepared to lead in any economy and circumstance. There is a beautiful old warrior mantra that states: 'The more you sweat in training, the less you bleed in battle.' I have lived by this mantra every single day.

The crisis shows the state of leadership inside the organization. At all levels, companies are short on the quantity and quality of leaders they need. There's no shortage of raw talent. We need to move beyond traditional leadership development practices to transform people who believe in their innate quality to lead. Only then can we see more people at every level of the organization deliver the best results, no matter what. It is then that every organization will succeed, and every individual will win at their game. *'If you desire to make a difference in the world, you must be different from the world.'*—Elaine S. Dalton.

---

## THE NINE LAWS

I tell my clients, 'Winning, winning, winning.' Most people run from winning because they are afraid of what comes with winning; the stress, the responsibility, the work. But I believe winning keeps you sharp, it challenges you in ways you never imagined and forces you to do your best in situations that send other people running for cover.

And so, through this book, I feel fortunate to share with you how to flip failures to wins. How you can win the leadership game every time.

My father would often remind me that everything in the universe is guided by an order, a methodological arrangement. Just as a seed doesn't struggle to become a tree—it simply unfolds in grace; you too can win the leadership game with grace and ease. I believe laws guide us to order our lives and ourselves. They are powerful principles; they set you on a direct course to authentically achieve your goals when put into practice.

The purpose of these nine laws is to guide you to win the leadership game methodologically.

Very often, the unpredictable nature of crises means that leaders have no time to prepare. During an emergency, everybody looks to a leader for the next step or reassurance. If a leader projects fear and unease, that unease transmits to everyone else, much like a contagious disease. Who then can the leader look up to for support?

Sadly, our business world portrays leaders as solid and perfect, who can withstand all pain and challenges. True that when you take up a leadership role, you sign up for challenges and blame. But leaders face exhaustion and burnout just like anyone else. How leaders react during the crisis and burnout is what decides their leadership quality. You need to depend on yourself the most if you want to win every time. And the laws in this book are written for the same purpose.

For the past 21 years, I have worked with millions of people around the world. Few of them go on to be super successful. Most do not. There are nine simple yet powerful laws that these super successful leaders apply in their lives that others do not. If you learn and apply these laws in your daily life, you will know how to play and win the leadership game. Each law in this book I've learned from some of the most successful and influential people in the world. I've practiced them sincerely in my one life and I stand true testimony to the heights it has taken me and my work and the fulfillment it has given me.

What I am giving you in this book is an insight into the thinking and practices of those who have found unparalleled success at their work. These laws will help you get into action. It will change forever the way you look at people and relationships at work. These laws will force you to go inside of yourself and bring about a significant transformation in yourself. It will encourage you to change yourself so that more people wish to connect with you.

As you read this book, you will discover that winning in leadership is not about blowing off someone else's candle but about lighting up someone's spirit. It's not about position or titles but about making a difference wherever you are. It's about knowing how to inspire people to do what you wish to accomplish. You will discover how to be a catalyst and change people's lives across the world in ways you can ever imagine. You will begin to trust yourself and your potential. You will develop a high tolerance for frustration, disappointment, and failure, of which you will recover quickly because you know that you could be betrayed and envied and that this is part of the leadership game. Winning people take risks and go for their dreams and goals; they conquer the objectives and, at the same time, have the ability, innate or acquired, to strengthen themselves when something does not go as planned.

Now is the time to learn and apply the laws in this book. Don't wait until you are finished reading all the laws before you take action. As soon as you read one habit, begin to apply it and see the changes it brings into your thinking, action, and behavior. This book is about helping you raise your game and win the leadership game. It's about assisting organizations in getting more of their people to play to win so that the people succeed, organizations grow, and the country's economy increases.

The book is here to help gain momentum, be a winner, and break through to the top of the pyramid. Now let me tell you something interesting here. This book is here to get you to be the person who plays to win every day. It will transform you into a leader who can look ahead, anticipate what is coming and move quickly and adjust to any new reality. It will get you to be a leader who is better able to meet challenges than others are.

And as you begin to see that transformation in yourself, and as you start to create an impact in the lives of people just like I do, I want you to know that I believe in your innate quality to lead and influence, regardless of your title and circumstance.

And while you play to win, there will be many instances where you will fall and fail. It's a part of the game, and it's necessary. The idea is that you get back on track soon and still play to win until you last in the game. That's what winning is all about—being in the game with the enthusiasm of winning every time. Winning is about speed and serenity. Both are equally important in the leadership game.

These nine laws will help you get there and be in the game and play full-on. So that at the end of your game, when it's time for you to leave the platform and hand it over to someone else, you can look back and say to yourself, 'I won in every sense.' That smile that you have on your face at the end of it is what we all want ultimately in our career life—fulfillment.

# The Nine Laws to Win the Leadership Game

# 1

## Law of Gap

In my role as an executive coach, I've seen more professionals stuck in their careers than I've seen growing. Now growth is very subjective. It means different things to different people. For some, growth is all about positions and titles. For others, it's about the status quo and salary increase, while for some, it's about self-development. For a few others, it might mean getting more projects and more work. Everyone sees growth differently. Whatever growth means for you, one thing is clear; everyone wants to grow at their job. Or at least most people want to grow; they don't want to be stagnant. People want to reach where they want to be.

Have you ever longed to be somewhere different from where you are? Have you always known deep down in your heart that you are meant to be much more than you currently are? Trust me when I say IBT—I've been there. I know the discomfort of the gap. It took me a seven-year period to know that I wanted to start my own business and create it. And finally, the dream did come true. It took me even longer to live my calling of helping the workforce in India to become transformed leaders so that India would be seen as a country that develops world-class leaders. Waiting can be hard. Especially when you just don't know how long it will take for you to make your dream a reality and whether or not you will ever get there. That's unknown.

Whether you're waiting to hear back from that angel investor, waiting to find out if the dream client will accept your proposal, or waiting to hear from a top-pick potential hire who's choosing between you and your competitor, playing the waiting game is always hard. And waiting usually means worrying. As I write this book during the Covid-19 pandemic, I am talking with CEOs across different time zones, and I sense their worry about cash flow and liquidity because payments are not coming in, but expenses are on the rise. The wait for them is intense.

DOI: 10.4324/9781003260714-3

31

Like millions of people, you may find yourself repeatedly stuck in the same old rut in your career and life. Too often, we hold ourselves back from pursuing our hopes, aspirations, dreams, or purpose despite many of our personal and professional accomplishments, experience, and knowledge. I encourage you to think deeply about *what's holding you back to reach where you want to be?*

Over the years, I've learned that no matter what kind of goal someone is trying to achieve, no matter where they want to be in their career life— there is one common trap that keeps people from living their dreams. It's the 'gap trap.'

Just like how a rat is caught in a mousetrap, animals are caught in a trap set by hunters, or the fish caught in the net spread by the fisherman, we humans get caught in the gap trap. And the funny part is this trap isn't laid for us by someone else. We lay this trap for ourselves. It is no outsider but your own mind that lays the trap for you. You might have caught yourself obsessing over negative events that happened in the past or brooding over adverse circumstances. That's the trap.

The gap trap that your mind lays for you involves negative thought patterns that are immersive or repetitive. Then you become 'stuck' in negative ways of replaying past hurts without moving toward solutions or feelings of resolution.

Sharon, the editor of a luxury lifestyle magazine, dreams of owning her own publishing company. If you were to meet Sharon, you would say she is highly intellectual and loaded with charisma. She is known for her exceptional people skills. Her boss invites her to be a part of all sales meetings because of her persuasion skills. Sharon can inspire her team to work long hours without any complaints from them. She is highly creative when it comes to magazine content and design. For 17 years, she's been in this field of publishing. Yet, she isn't even close to her dream of owning her own publishing company. Why? Because in a couple of incidents, she messed up some huge client deals that cost the company substantial dollar amounts. So whenever she thinks about her dream of opening her firm, her mind acts like her faithful servant and brings forth the memories of those failed deals and projects. And what follows is Sharon continuously telling herself, 'I am still not mature enough to handle this.' Her pattern of thoughts doesn't generate new ways of thinking, new behaviors, or new possibilities. She only goes over the same information repeatedly without change and stays negative, adding on more self-destructive thoughts.

Her mind has created the gap trap, which isn't allowing her to get from where she is to where she wants to be. For most of us, this gap trap exists. It's an internal one.

Articulating a vision is a leader's birthright. We love to dream and create. The challenge is in reaching there. That gap between where we are and where we want to go seems so large that the majority of us get overwhelmed just thinking about the gap. And so, we give up. And then we try to run away from that goal, from the dream, believing we aren't made for greatness.

Myles Munroe said that the world's wealthiest places were not the oil wells of Saudi Arabia or the diamond fields in South Africa but the graveyard. He considered the graveyard the richest place in the world, harboring those who die without realizing their potential.

People die with unfinished careers, unwritten books, songs not written and composed, and houses not designed. It makes me ask questions—can one have it all? Can I be all-am-designed to be? Is there such a thing as a purpose for life? I don't know. But I know that if you have a dream, a goal, or a purpose, you must begin your journey toward it. No one knows the end of this journey or where we will reach. What's important is that to win the leadership game, you must begin playing the game.

I have read about people who, at 40, decide to pursue entirely new career paths. I had read about people who, at 55, chose to live life differently—the way they felt they ought to have when they were 25. And I have witnessed people at 29 give up in life.

The law of the gap says that gaps will always exist in some parts of your life. You can't control or anticipate every gap that will come your way. You can control how you respond to the gap and your ability to fill that gap. Some people adjust themselves to the gap, some adjust the gap to themselves, some wait for you to tell them how to close the gap, and some work out a plan to close it. Successful people don't wait and don't have one plan. They have every possible option available to close that gap every time it shows up in their life.

## THE CHAIR YOU CAN'T SIT ON

A client of mine, Jones, very recently told me a story about his father, a painter at heart but worked for 37 years selling kids' clothing in a department store in Texas. Due to the pandemic and lockdown effects, one day, he was told the store was closing. The management asked him if they could do anything for him; his only request was to have the chair he'd been sitting in all those years. They willingly gave it to him.

'He brought that chair to my house on his back one day,' Jones said, 'and placed it in my living room and told me about all the years he sat in it, about how he could have played big by going out there and becoming one of the best painters ever on this planet. And then he made me promise that I would never sit down in that chair, ever. It's in my living room to this day, and I never sit in it.'

Let me ask you this; is there a chair you are sitting on with all your dreams and ideas?

Marianne Williamson: 'Our deepest fear is not that we're inadequate; our deepest fear is that we're powerful beyond measure.' Few people can adapt on the fly and make quick decisions that give results.

## BRIDGE THE GAP

On a family vacation to London, I came across the words 'mind the gap' at the London Underground metro system. It's a safety announcement, advising passengers to be careful when stepping across the opening between train doors and station platforms. I was fascinated with these words. I found this phrase very powerful, reminding all of us that there will never be a time in your life, both professionally and personally, where the gap will not exist. Even the most outstanding achievers I've met and interacted with acknowledge a gap between where they are and where they want to be. Most of us are not conscious of the gap. We ignore it. I have observed most people give up mid-way and feel the gap is too large to close. Listen to me very carefully. It's your leadership breakthrough moment. No gap in your life is so large that you cannot bridge it. The reason it seems overwhelming is that we view the gap as a tunnel rather than a bridge. There's a difference between going through something and going to some-thing. When you're going to something, you're on the bridge. You are full of hope to get to the other end. It's a happy journey. When you're going through something, you're in a tunnel—wondering that there's some light at the end of the tunnel. You want to come out of that darkness desperately, and the journey seems like hell.

The question you need to ask yourself is this: Is my attitude toward the gaps in my life a tunnel or a bridge? To win in the leadership game, you must develop a bridge attitude where you see yourself as going toward your destination over a bridge that you build with your self-discipline and persistence. It will help you overcome the challenges and obstacles that you will face in your journey to close the gap. It will get you to some of the brilliant opportunities you need to get to the other end of the bridge.

The reason why most people see the gap as a tunnel is because of their thinking. If you are anxious to close the gap and change your circumstances, you must be willing to make a bridge between the gap of where you are and where you want to go. And this bridge is first crossed inside of you. You can reduce the gap by your power to think. Thinking is the most incredible power you have to close any gap in your career life. It all depends on how and what you think. Many people play small in their career life because they limit their thinking. And so, the gap between where they are and where they want to go is never bridged.

And Rajneesh Jain, CFO of Reliance, explains this so well when he says that what got him and the organization so far was the ability to think big. On one of my podcast episodes, I had the opportunity to talk with Rajneesh, and that's when I heard him advocate the think big principle. And then, I approached him to share more about this principle, and here's what he said. He said,

> Payal, not being afraid to take on new challenges and assignments, as overwhelming they might appear, has helped me gain the rich experience that got me here. To begin with, the ability to think big in itself is not the bottleneck in one's personal and professional growth. The fear of daring to think big keeps individuals and leaders from achieving heights in their lives. And I believe the lack of vision and a plan fuels that fear. To break down the above, I believe the ingredients for thinking big consist of (a) having a risk-taking mindset, where one is not afraid to imagine and then take on the seemingly impossible assignments, and (b) having a long-term vision with a clearly defined path and goals. Both of these complement each other, and having the right balance of the two is what gets one going. And one thing I have learned from my experiences of successful executions is that focusing on details is the make-or-break parameter. I believe the work done

by Shri Mukesh Ambani, Indian billionaire businessman and the chairman, managing director, and largest shareholder of Reliance Industries Ltd., itself epitomizes the concept of thinking big.

As I heard Rajneesh talk about the think big principle, I was curious to know what Shri Mukesh Ambani and his team did that led to Reliance being more successful than ever. I questioned Rajneesh more. I wanted to pick the brain of this person who is instrumental in the success story of Reliance; Rajneesh said with complete conviction,

> Payal, the launch and growth of Jio in the Indian market have been a testimony to the concept of think big. Jio launched with a mammoth ambition of connecting everyone in India, providing them with the internet experience, and gradually making India a forerunner in the Digital Society. The success of Jio validates how thinking big can lead to achieving the seemingly impossible success for an individual, business, corporate, or society in general. The vision of Hon'ble Prime Minister Shri Narendra Modi to create a Digital India way back in 2014 shows how Governments also can benefit from the power of thinking big and creating a more inclusive society. I want to conclude by quoting Shri Dhirubhai Ambani here—'Think big, think fast, think ahead. Ideas are no one's monopoly.'

Rajneesh and the entire Reliance team are a true testimony of how our ability to think big is one of the major ways to close the gap in our career lives.

Few people can think big. Most of us compromise our thinking by listening to what others have to say about us. We define our growth based on their opinion. When I coach high-end executives, we try many new things because they're so dedicated to their growth that we have the time and latitude to experiment with different ideas. And because we are thinking big, we can fill that gap. The way to bridge the gap is to expand your thinking and then execute that thinking. And the starting point is by being aware of the gap.

Being aware of the gap and taking action helps you evaluate yourself and the different aspects of your life. What's my income situation right now? How's my leadership? Where am I on my career growth? And on and on.

Being aware of the gap consists of two significant elements.

#1 Where are you in your career now?

Where are you in your career ?

Where you want to be in your career ?

**FIGURE 1.1**
The Think Big Bridge

#2 Where do you want to be in your career?

Now this gap between where you are and where you want to be is bridged by the process of thinking big.

Here's something I want to encourage you to practice, so you can take action to fill the gap in your life. I want you to work on the below exercise step by step.

Step 1: Critically assess your current situation. Pick one area of your career life where the gap exists? Now write down where you are right now in that area of your career life. For instance, what's my income situation right now? How's my leadership? Where am I on my career growth? And on and on. It may be obvious, or it may require a great deal of introspection.

Step 2: Determine your desired vision: Now, see where you want to be in that area of your career life and write that down. Clearly being able to identify this will make it easier to set a goal and take action.

Step 3: Assess the gap: The dotted line in the diagram is the gap you want to bridge between where you are and where you want to be. This is the space where you are and where you want to be.

Step 4: Commit to moving ahead: Now, list all the actions you must take to bridge the gap. These actions may also include removing barriers both internal and external.

Step 5: Re-assess the gap: Every three months, revisit this practice and check which actions you've completed and where you currently are on bridging the gap. Check how much of the gap you've been able to bridge.

This practice will propel you forward. Don't be afraid to experiment. Set aside time weekly to reflect on this exercise. Use your reflections to help keep you on track—making adjustments as necessary for the following week.

## WHY EXECUTION IS A LEADER'S GREATEST CHALLENGE?

There are two kinds of people I've met in the professional field. One who constantly thinks, 'I don't feel like doing it right now.' This group of people lets their emotions and feelings dominate their actions. They wait until they feel good to act. If you wait until you feel ready to tackle something challenging, you might be waiting a long time. It's unlikely that you're going to gain a sudden burst of inspiration out of the blue. The majority of the people fall into this group. The second group of people is the ones who say, 'I will do it so I can feel better.' This group believes that their actions will lead to a sense of fulfillment internally. They use motion to change their emotion. Let me tell you they are in the minority. Most of us commit to action only if we feel a certain level of motivation. And we feel motivation only when we feel enough emotional inspiration.

Before the pandemic hit the world, I met Akansha, an entrepreneur who supplied paper products to restaurants. When the economy was booming, so was her business. She had a few great clients to whom she would provide the products and get some good income. Once I asked her about her future business plan, she said she wanted to grow the business and be more known in the industry. I asked her if she had started working on the same, and her answer is something I still remember. She said, 'I will work on it when the time is right. As of now, things are going great with my current clients.' Now, I am not saying that one must not focus on the current clients or not be satisfied with what you have got. It amuses me that people have extraordinary dreams and plans but ordinary habits that don't allow them to win. Waiting for the right time means waiting forever. I met Akansha again during the pandemic and asked her the same question about how things were in business for her and her future business plan, and this time around, she answered saying, 'it's just not the right time for this Payal. The business has slowed down considerably, and I am barely making a living.' Her situation was terrible.

My point here is that the reason why the gap doesn't close for many, the reason we find ourselves stuck in a rut is because of the time we take from ideation to execution. Our ordinary habits prevent us from achieving our extraordinary dreams. If Akansha would have executed her ideas parallelly during the boom period rather than being complacent with her current clients, things would've been much better for her during the pandemic.

Here's your leadership breakthrough moment. Every minute, every hour, every day that you spend around waiting to do what you want to do, someone else is already doing it.

So, while you are trying to decide whether or not you should act, someone else has already acted. While you are only saying what you will do, someone out there has begun doing it. The most successful people are those with instincts to respond quickly to situations and take the appropriate actions while avoiding being negligent.

One of the challenges I've seen people face while wanting to give it their best is their old habits.

I was once attending a conference where I had to present for 30 minutes a leadership talk. Before me, there were some presenters. I vividly remember this one presenter who said a statement at least three times in the introduction of her speech. She said, 'I don't want to be a talking head who only talks but does not engage her audience. I want to have a two-way dialogue with you so I can help you.' Now that's a great statement, and if speakers can get their audience to engage with them during the session, it's a 100% success. I was impressed. As she began her talk, I observed she did precisely what she did not want to do. She was a talking head who kept talking about her life, her struggles, her success, and the tools she applied in her life. Do you see the gap here between what she wanted to do and what she did in reality?

Ordinary habits prevent us from achieving our extraordinary goals, so the gap in our life seems hard to fill. Execution is hard. It takes focus, buy-in, and the biggest challenge of all: changes in our habits.

I know of so many companies that offer a particular budget to the employees to join courses and be a speaker at various industry events. Did you know that barely 7% of the employees avail of that benefit? It is ordinary habits that prevent us from achieving extraordinary results.

One of the biggest challenges people worldwide face is filling the gap between where they are and where they want to achieve execution excellence. Execution is an emotion regulation problem, not a time management problem. We don't execute not because of lack of resources or skills but because we cannot cope with challenging emotions and negative moods induced by specific tasks—boredom, anxiety, insecurity, frustration, resentment, self-doubt, self-sabotaging, and beyond. Guess what, IBT— I've been there.

During the early years of business, my father would often check on me to see how things were going. When I would tell him of all the excuses that things could not be done while blaming it on the culture, the environment, the economy, or simply procrastinating because of that overwhelming feeling, here's what he would say: 'don't just sit there. Do something. The answers will follow.' Maybe it is because of this practice that I have been able to keep going ahead with new ideas to help leaders and organizations today while in a pandemic situation. In those early days of establishing my company, I remember if I had to redesign an entire website, I'd force myself to sit down and would say, 'Okay, I'll just design the header right now.' But after I worked on the header, I'd find myself moving on to other parts of the site. And before I knew it, I'd be energized and engaged in the project.

I once heard about a novelist who had written over 70 novels. Someone asked the novelist how he was able to write so consistently and remain inspired and motivated. He replied, 'Two hundred crappy words per day, that's it.' The idea was that if he forced himself to write two hundred crappy words, more often than not, the act of writing would inspire him, and before he knew it, he'd have thousands of words down on the page.

It is Nolan Bushnell who said that everyone who's ever taken a shower has an idea. It's the person who gets out of the shower, dries off, and does something about it who makes a difference. While great ideas are needed to create a successful startup, the factors that determine long-term success and the ability to scale up the business are execution. Execution matters. Execution is what fills the gap between where you are and where you want to be. Execution: It is the ability to get things done, no matter what, to get results, and to keep moving forward despite the challenges, hardships, and obstacles that lay ahead. Your speed of execution will decide if you are a winner or an average player.

Here's what I want to tell you—do something. That 'something' can be a minor viable action toward something else. It can be anything. If you just take one tiny winy step to start what you've been pushing off, I promise you this you will feel inspired to take another action and then another and then another. And in the process, you will fall and fail, but that is a part of the process. And by the time you know it, chances are you'll end up somewhere entirely different from what you thought.

I've never thought of myself as a writer. But, if you'd told me that night three years ago that I'd have been a New York award-winning author and writing more leadership books, I probably would have choked on a taco. But, by taking action one step at a time, that's where I've ended up.

## FROM IDEATION TO EXECUTION

Your micro-actions will lead you to your macro goals. I say to my clients that every night before going to bed, ask yourself a simple question, 'did I do my best today?' Your honest answer will help you improve your game daily.

Surprisingly, the biggest obstacle to achieving your dreams and goals isn't the gap at all but failing to see a bridge that will take you where you want to go. The universe delivers a series of continuous human experiences that help us fill that gap, but we fall into the gap trap.

The gap in your life is not meant to scare you, stop you, or hold you back. It's intended to wake you up and shake you up, preparing you to move toward where you want to go. I believe with certainty that there's no gap seemingly more significant than the one between where you are right now and where you want to be. What's needed is execution. Most of us get stuck at the ideation level.

Having spent two decades of my career helping leaders recognize and overcome their leadership challenges in almost every industry globally, it's easy for me to identify limiting patterns. From working with top CEOs to university students, the same problem exists across all categories—lack of execution.

We have more productivity gurus, apps, education, and information than ever before, yet why are we unable to execute our ideas with speed? It's because we've forgotten the golden rule of business—rely on yourself the most. Today there is a plethora of information available, and this information confuses us more than it helps us. And for that reason, we get trapped in this net of information, which has adverse effects on us. Rather than allowing us to act on our plans and decisions, it slows us down, confuses us, makes us procrastinate, and we wait endlessly for things to change. In today's business era, you've got to rely on yourself and know yourself because you take yourself with you everywhere. As much as we enjoy blaming externally for the lack of our actions, we all know that execution is a power that comes from within us at the end of the day. No one, not even the pandemic, can stop you from taking action if you want to.

We don't go from ideation to execution because we fail to elevate and evaluate ourselves from the inside. We've forgotten to trust ourselves. We blame everyone and everything without realizing that we have been blessed with the power to act.

I was recently giving a presentation to a small group of entrepreneurs when one of the attendees said,

> I've struggled here too long. I think I'll just move to Silicon Valley; then, I can set up a new venture, meet new people and set new goals for my business. Someone else spoke up and said, 'Nice plan, but you'd still have to go with you.'

So true. You can run away from everything but not yourself. For so many people, the gap between where they are and where they want to seems so large that they do everything to close it, except the most important thing—work on themselves. You are the common factor in your life and, no matter where you go, what you do, or whom it is that you hang out with, you still have to be there. You take that gap with you everywhere. If you don't change, all the machinations in the world aren't going to help.

For this fellow intent on moving to Silicon Valley, the change is not about the venue; the difference is about choosing to be a great entrepreneur now. That imperative is internal, not situational and, when we recognize it as internal, we foster the shift in an experience that we seek. As I mentioned earlier in this chapter, the gap you face in your life is not external; it's internal.

Recently David was suffering from anxiety disorder and wasn't able to focus on his work. For the past three years, he had been working on a project that could get him to become the company's director. However, the position got filled by an external candidate, and Joe's current role continued. For five and a half years, he has been aspiring for the role of the director, but it did not happen for him. This experience made David feel like a failure. The gap between his current managerial role and his aspiring director role seemed too large internally than externally because David was broken internally. And he shrunk inside, which got him to believe the gap externally was too large.

Being aware of the gap helps you evaluate yourself and the different aspects of your life. What's my income situation right now? How's my leadership? Where am I on my career growth? And on and on.

Being aware of the gap consists of two significant elements. The diagram below explains it.

No matter what level of your career you're at, I believe you've probably experienced something like this. Remember this my friend, if you desire to live a mission-driven life, if you want to close the gaps in your life, and if you wish to be great at execution, the first step is to look within you. If the gap inside of you is large, you will never be able to fill that gap externally; however, small it may be in reality. Usually, we ourselves weave the trap of a gap by our negative thoughts and emotions. Gap traps are irrational thought patterns that blind you to the truth, causing you to make errors in judgment. As you become more conscious of your gap traps, you learn that each one is a combined exaggeration of a threat and an underestimation of your ability to deal with it. Gap traps limit possibilities and undermines your resources to cope with inevitable challenges. It stresses you out, and soon you begin to believe that you can't reach the place where you want to, and that you are not cut for winning. And so, you start to settle for less.

There have been times in my life where I have felt 'rock bottom.' I thought I wasn't made for success and that I could never do anything impactful in my professional life. Negative thoughts and feelings about myself and my work struggles would take over entirely, and as a result, I remained caught in the gap trap, making poor choices. But something inside of me told me to move ahead. I would continuously hear a voice that would push me as if it were saying to me—keep moving ahead. I knew I had to break the gap trap and realize my potential.

They say that a journey of a thousand miles begins with a single step, and that first step can be one of the hardest things you ever do. Uncertainty, moments of self-doubt, judgment from friends and family, I faced it all when I was on my journey to growth and winning. But here's your leadership breakthrough moment—if you take that first step anyway, because you believe in your ideas and, even more importantly, you believe in yourself, you will eventually get there. I came out of the gap trap and built a coaching and training empire that is recognized worldwide. I began writing books on leadership and soon got recognized as the only woman of Indian descent to be a leadership speaker and author in a white male-dominated industry. And since then, I've helped a million people make the often chal-lenging journey from where they are in life to where they want to be.

Yes, it's possible. I am an ordinary woman who chooses to make extraor-dinary choices daily. It's my mantra for winning. My clients have embraced this mantra for their win. What about you?

The only way you, me, or anyone can come out of the gap trap is by going from the ideation phase to the execution phase. Action isn't just the effect of motivation; it's also the cause of it. You don't need to find divine inspir-ation to start feeling motivated.

Remember you can't control or anticipate every gap that might come your way. You can only control your response. You can become your source of inspiration. You can become your source of motivation. Action is always within reach. And with simply doing something as your only metric for success—well, then even failure pushes you forward. Whatever happens, however large the gap, you have the power and smarts to bridge the gap and achieve the desired outcome.

## RAPID ACTION PLAN

Make a list of actions you know you must take to fill the gap between where you are and where you want to be. Now pick one action, only one action from that list, and execute it before you read the next law.

# 2

## Law of Mastery

What does mastery of leadership mean to you? Look, if you want to win the leadership game, you have to be a master at the game. To different people, it is mastery of other things: mastery of the skill, mastery of strategic planning, mastery of consistent achievements. When I think about mastery, I remember there's a story about the famous artist, Picasso which I read many years back.

*A woman came up to him and asked him to sketch something on a piece of paper. He sketched it and gave it back to her, saying: 'That will cost you $10,000.' She was astounded. 'You took just five minutes to do the sketch,' she said. Isn't $10,000 a lot for five minutes of work?*

*'The sketch may have taken me five minutes, but the learning took me 30 years,' Picasso retorted.*

Winning is less about natural talent and more about the mastery of your craft.

Here's my take on this law. Mastery is your genius point. And to win the leadership game every time, you've got to reach your genius point. Doing your job is the easy part. While many people can complete routine tasks, meet company standards, and ensure customers are satisfied, they often fail at mastering their crafts. Winning doesn't happen because you finish your day-to-day tasks. Winning requires you to be a master in your craft. Ask yourself, am I a master in your field?

I define mastery with the help of this simple equation.

Daily Practice + Skills + Dedication + Focus = Mastery

Almost everyone wants to achieve success. It seems to be an inextricable part of the human experience. We have that unshakable yearning to be considered among the best in the world. Success, whatever your definition of the word might be, requires mastery.

DOI: 10.4324/9781003260714-4

The intensity of practice defines the pace and degree of skill. Whatever your role is in a business, one of your top goals should always be to master your craft. When we become too comfortable with ourselves, mastery dwindles, and our skills become stagnant. Mastering your craft makes you not only more marketable to the industry you're in but also better at what you're already doing. It requires daily practice and effort.

*As a young salesperson, Raj read every book, listened to every bit of audio, attended every training session, and reached out to every mentor he could find. He succeeded in his line of work, was promoted faster than any of his peers, and was awarded the best salesperson for seven consecutive years because the other salespeople he competed against were going to their jobs and doing their job. Instead of mastering the craft of selling, they fell into the daily routines of their jobs, target numbers, and settled for what they had.*

Most of us don't achieve a high level of mastery that takes us to our genius point because our ideas about mastery tend to be externalized. Our training, development, and educational systems have helped us fill-up the container of knowledge and give us tons of information but rarely help us reach our genius point. With the best of the training we receive at our workplace, 75% of the organization comprises what I call 'trained' leaders.

## WILL YOU BE A TRAINED LEADER OR A TRANSFORMED LEADER?

Years ago, one of my clients, a Chief Human Resource Officer, wanted me to help him create a culture of what I am an expert at, developing transformed leaders in his organization. I talked to him about my Unstoppable Leader Workshop, a transformed leadership development program that helps managers change their behavior from the inside. Once that is attained, everything and anything is possible in a person's life.

The program, along with its other components, consists of a pre-group meeting with the potential managers who were being considered for various roles in the company. During the session, I noticed that they were all great at their functional skills. They had received more than needed leadership training yet weren't even close to being a transformed leaders. They were well-trained leaders. Now you may ask, Payal, what is the definition of a transformed leader? Is it enough to have years of experience, a degree from a top-notch university, work diligently, and have an impressive title? No: especially not in today's complex, ever-evolving digital workplace. In the introduction chapter of this book, I had introduced you to the concept of a transformed leader and its importance in winning the leadership game every time. Let me talk to you more about this.

The difference between trained leaders and transformed leaders begins long before they assume the mantle of leadership. A person can be a transformed leader even if they do not have a leadership title or position.

How is that possible? Because transformed leadership begins from within. As leaders, we receive recognition for our external mastery: revenue, profit, new products, and market share. The core questions here are as follows: Where do the external results come from? 'What is the foundation to the most effective, results-producing leaders? What supports their various competencies or styles on the surface?' It's them as a person. We lead by virtue of who we are.

You see, leaders are everywhere. Trained leaders are plenty. Transformed leaders are rare. Figure 2.1 will show you the difference in the thinking and behavior pattern of a trained leader v/s transformed leader.

Trained leaders have skills and functional expertise but their actions fall short because of their limiting thinking and beliefs. Transformed leaders on the other hand go beyond skills and project themselves in ways that show they are here to make a difference come what may.

Maximum people operate on average because they are content with being trained leaders. The journey to becoming a transformed leader isn't something that just happens overnight. It takes time, courage, failure, struggle,

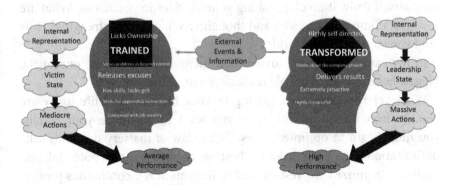

**FIGURE 2.1**
Trained v/s Transformed Leader

patience, and discipline. Who's willing to put themselves through all of the pain and failure when there's an easier way out? Being a transformed leader means you have a more profound desire for greatness and personal achievement. To be a master in your craft, you've got to think like a transformed leader.

Those who aim for mastery in their craft, for them, nothing matters more than their work.

Not fame. Not fortune. Not glory. It's their true love, their greatest passion. I remember, in my #askpayal where leaders from across the world send me their questions, I received a question from a rising musician. He asked me to be a musician who receives name, fame, and accolades for his work. The answer to his question is still available on my YouTube channel. What I told him was very close to my heart. While name, fame, and accolades are agile, work is not. Work is the only constant while you are struggling and while it seems you've made it. You will be remembered for your work. Every master was a beginner in their field and worked every day with discipline to achieve great heights in their field. Their brains function differently because winning comes naturally to them. As simple as this law of mastery may sound, it's one of the hardest to practice. But there is a powerfully simple way to achieve mastery.

## GO INSIDE TO GROW OUTSIDE

Being a transformed leader begins with the will and commitment to work on yourself daily. It involves asking yourself questions, such as: What are my most dominant emotions and thoughts? What are my strengths? How am I showing up in the world?

In my experience as an advisor and mentor to executives, one of the biggest failures I see in people is a lack of self-optimization.

Whatever results you are getting in your business and life today are coming from inside of you. So if you want to maximize your results, you must begin to optimize yourself—the law of mastery demands self-optimization. One must make the best use of their abilities, potential, and skills to maximize their results. Self-optimization is a continuous process where you focus on becoming the best version of yourself daily. It's a process of having a clear understanding of your emotions and how you react to difficult situations. It's about understanding the 'triggers' and 'stressors' in your life and having a plan for processing stress and disappointment. It's about staying curious and trying to take regular steps to learn more about yourself. So if you have been practicing self-optimization, when you receive criticism, you will ask: 'How can I learn from this experience?' rather than getting triggered negatively by the complaint.

The more often you can apply this sort of introspective approach to your professional life, the more it will benefit your leadership—and your team.

You see few leaders being able to be masters in their field because these few leaders have been optimizing themselves daily. And to optimize yourself, you have to go inside. You see, so many of us have a broken perspective of both our interior and our exterior selves. How many times have you told yourself statements like?

- I'm not good at my work.
- I am an introvert.
- I am not good at connecting with people.
- I am always at fault here.
- What a failure I am.
- I am destined to be average.
- I sound like an idiot when I give suggestions.
- My ideas will not be appreciated.
- I'm never getting ahead in my work.

Sound familiar? I see it every day with people—leaders work with a sense of disappointment that they aren't motivating their teams enough. Individuals at work feel broken when they lose out on a promotion. We often underestimate ourselves and overestimate others.

Some years back, I was coaching a senior manager who worked at Uber and faced the challenge of growing in the organization. With a lot of hard work and dedication, she reached this far. But now, for the past seven years, she has been stuck in the mid-management role. During the coaching sessions, I learned that she had confidence issues when dealing with people in higher positions than her. Fear, tension, and nervousness took over her when she was in a meeting with senior leaders. All of this led her not to share suggestions, and she often failed to articulate her ideas well. Because of this, she would often be passed over for promotion.

I asked her to practice a simple technique called Flip It Now (FIN). It's a simple technique where you pick one of your negative, limiting scripts, toss it in the air with a question, replace it with the new answer you get and then apply the new script. So, she took her old script of 'I can't confidently speak out in meetings with my senior management and tossed it in the air with the question—"What is that one thing I am great at regarding my leadership ability?"' She answered it by picking her ability to mentor others. She was great at guiding people and was an excellent listener. So, instead of feeling fearful at the meeting and disregarding her ideas as stupid, she chose to look at herself as a mentor in the discussions, which became a game changer for her. As a mentor, she focused more on listening, asking questions, being nonjudgmental, being knowledgeable, and giving constructive feedback. She began replacing her old script with the new. The more she applied the new hand, the easier it became to connect with anyone she wanted to.

What would happen if you flipped the script inside of you? In other words: 'What would happen if you pick one thing that you like about yourself-something you are great at?'

FIN technique is based on the law of awareness that means to go inside. Going inside yourself means to process information in the context of what you believe, how you think, how you feel, or what your intuitive senses are telling you. It would help if you gained a firm understanding of your core philosophies, values, personal beliefs, and preconceived biases. It means that we have an opportunity to do the 'inner work' to reflect on what we can control and how we can move things forward.

Successful leaders ask themselves this one question every morning—do I like who I am today? And they answer this question not based on their titles, position, accomplishments, or wealth, but with a deep reflection of who they indeed are. They shut themselves from the outside voice so that they could hear their inner voice. They do a self-inventory each day of who they are and whether or not they like who they are. Because until you are fully aware of who you are, you cannot upgrade yourself. To win, you must be mindful of yourself.

Before you read ahead, I want you to experiment with this exercise I call Creating an Imaginary You.

I want you to pretend for a second that you are someone completely different from who you are right now. If you could be someone else, what would you be? How would this person act, think, and behave? What would be the routine of this person? What would the personality be like? Would you be an introvert or an extrovert? What would your gifts and talents be? What would your strengths be?

Now, think about this imaginary person you've concocted. Is this person like you in any way? Or did you create someone utterly opposite from yourself that you don't even recognize?

I have news for you—that person you wish you were, is your true self. That person needs to be created in reality. And the creator this time is not the Universe God or any higher power. This time the creator is YOU.

You are capable of making the most significant transformation of your life. And this transformation happens only when you step inside yourself to be aware of your authentic self.

In the business world, this is more important than ever because you are constantly dealing with various people and situations. Self-aware individuals can perceive their thoughts and feelings and 'read' others and the way they are recognized and perceived by them.

When dealing with people, especially those you label as complex people, always remind yourself that the problem is you. Which means the solution is also you. Successful people are constantly aware of what's inside of them.

## THE BLIND SPOTS

Part of my job as a parent was to serve as an initial driving instructor for my older teenage daughter. As part of the lesson, I demonstrated the reality of blind spots. I'd get out of the car to stand along the right side of the car and ask her if she could see me in the mirror. She would say, 'mom, you are invisible, though I can hear you.' I would then explain to her how while driving, there are often vehicles on our right and left whom we cannot see because they are in our blind spots that pose a significant danger. As a driver, it's super crucial for you to know where the blind spots are on your vehicle and other drivers' vehicles. Knowing this will help protect you and those around you from an easily avoidable accident. I taught her how to check her blind spots by simply looking over her shoulder to make sure these spots were clear before changing lanes.

The term blind spot is regularly used in leadership. Most people use it to refer to an unrecognized weakness or a threat that can undermine their growth and success. Many believe that great leaders are without any blind spots. As an executive coach, I can tell you that the higher up you are in the corporate hierarchy, the more your blind spots. It's because you are more likely to overrate yourself and develop blind spots that hinder your effectiveness. Hence, it's essential to recognize your blind spots. What are your blind spots in life and your leadership style?

I define blind spots as a set of behaviors—both self-destructive and self-healing behaviors. A blind spot is something about yourself, both negative and positive, and about your actions that you don't see clearly or are afraid to acknowledge. Everyone has blind spots, whether we recognize them or not. The problem is that it's easy to see another person's blind spots and not our own. And because of this, there are a lot of issues at our workplace. Personal and professional relations get negatively impacted because we see other people's blind spots, not our own. You cannot optimize yourself if you don't pay close attention to your blind spots.

One evening as I was walking out of the yoga class, I saw a man at the counter arguing with the receptionist over his class payments. Here's the backstory of the argument. The lady at the reception had wrongly billed the client $550/for one class instead of $55. So when the payment process was complete, and the client was walking out the door, checking the bill, when he saw the error and came back to the reception. He got angry with her for the mistake and blamed her for being irresponsible. In response, the reception got angry, blaming him for not checking the amount before swiping his card. This further led to an argument between the two of them. Let me ask you this—according to you, whose fault was it? Was the receptionist wrong or the client? Honestly, it doesn't matter. It doesn't matter who was right or wrong. What matters is how you handle the situation. Both took it in ways where it led to more anger and blame. This is what happens in our corporate world too. Our inability to manage our emotions at that time leads to responses that are detrimental to us and our work.

As a leadership development expert, I work with our corporate clients to build cultures that increase the number of transformed leaders. I believe this promotes growth, innovation, and robust results. One of the significant challenges people face in becoming a transformed leader is to optimize their emotions. For example, your ability to stay calm and not lose your temper when dealing with an overbearing manager or with a challenging employee requires you to divert some of your emotions so you can think strategically. Let me give you a real-life incident here. Two directors from different verticals in a startup organization were working alongside the same project. They each overhear their team members discussing a meeting with the union representative. One director interrupts the discussions, warning them that they might have to say goodbye to their work if they associate with any union. The other director realizes she doesn't know much about this and why the team felt the need to approach the union. Instead of reacting on the spot, she reviewed the company's website and labor laws. She learns about the appropriate steps and does the needful. The second director uses the principle of Metacognition. Metacognition means thinking about thinking. It's a process where you teach yourself to think in the best possible way. It's about the 3 W's—what you think, why you think, and when. It's a skill every individual in the organization must build top-down and must build. Too often, thinking has been seen as the exclusive domain of senior leaders and CEO. However, I've observed that when thinking becomes a daily practice of each person in the organization, it builds a culture of self-directed leaders. Remember, what sets apart the 20% of people in the organization from the rest is their thinking ability. People who win think differently. Period. They don't feel right or wrong. Just differently.

The increasingly complex nature of business means leaders need new skills to work with people from various cultural backgrounds. If we haven't practiced optimizing ourselves, it becomes tough to deal with the changes. And the most critical optimization is optimizing your emotions. It's the foundation of everything that happens to you.

*I recollect here a story I read about a young couple moving into a new neighborhood. The following day, while they are eating breakfast, the young woman sees her neighbor hang the wash outside. That laundry is not very clean, she said, she doesn't know how to wash correctly. Perhaps she needs better laundry soap. Her husband looked on but remained silent. Every time her neighbor would hang her wash to dry, the young woman would make the same comments. About one month later, the woman was surprised to see a nice clean wash on the line and said to her husband: 'Look! She has learned how to wash correctly. I wonder who taught her this.' The husband said: 'I got up early this morning and cleaned our windows!'*

It is not always easy to find that our window is clean or unclean. As in the story, we need external help to understand it. How do I get that help?

One of the practices I have personally found helpful in optimizing emotions is the process of metacognition. Metacognition is the art of stepping back from the situation and internally assessing your internal process. It's one of the most imperative ways to optimize your leadership. It takes great practice and consistency to develop this ability.

Think about this—have you ever consciously stepped back from an event or a situation to observe your thought and response consciously? It is easy to blame the other, someone else, or anyone else for our moods, actions, and words. But remember, finally, what we hold inside is all that will spill them out? And whatever you spill out will determine the direction of your results too. Most of us don't know what's inside of us. We don't look over our shoulders to spot our blind spots. That's why we blame people and situations.

Until you know the changes you need to make inside, you cannot grow on the outside. That means that leaders must hone in on who they are and what they desire to do to achieve growth. Have you ever sat down and reflected on your life and the person you are? Highly self-aware people have a habit of regularly reflecting on and considering their values. As our business world goes through the challenges of the Covid-19, the uncertainty, and the ever-changing business world, the law of self-optimization is most needed in every person in the corporate world. It seems to be in short supply among leaders. By knowing your values, personality, needs, habits, and emotions, and how they affect your actions and the actions of others, you'll be better able to manage your stress, make better decisions, and ultimately lead others to do the same.

The more aware you are of yourself, the more you increase your credibility as a leader. Teams led by self-aware leaders are less likely to experience internal conflict. Self-aware leaders are more likely to be high-performing, meet their business goals, and save on turnover costs.

I like what Mahatma Gandhi said, 'be the change you want to see in the world.' If you want to see an end to corruption, start by being scrupulously honest yourself. If you're going to see peace and love around you, begin within your own family. If you want people to treat you well, start by treating those around you with respect. If you care about the environment, start looking at your patterns of consumption and waste. Because at the end of it all, winning the leadership game is all about optimizing yourself to attain mastery in your craft.

---

## RAPID ACTION PLAN (RAP)

What one thing would you like to be known for in your industry? Identify ways in which you can be a master in your field.

# 3

## Law of Authenticity

Jasmine never really got along with her boss. She had become a target for sexual harassment and yet continued in the miserable job for over three years, tolerating the appalling behavior of her boss. One day she heard my *Power of I* talk organized by her company to celebrate women's day month. The talk completely changed her perspective. She understood that she had the power to change what she wanted and that no one except her was in control of her emotions. She looked back at her three years in the organization. She realized that she silently endured the ongoing sexual harassment from her new boss, tolerated unacceptable behavior from colleagues, and allowed the negativity of her team to shatter her from the inside. When she met with me after the session, she thanked me profoundly for the session, purchased all of my books, and parted saying, 'Payal, you know when someone close to me was feeling unsatisfied, negative, or in search of someone to blame, there I was, ready to take it. But no more.' Her smile told me she had changed from within. I will be honest here; I didn't do any magic. I only helped her recognize her authentic self.

During the Covid-19 crisis, most people had to work from home. Almost every day, I heard how frustrated people became with putting in more work hours from home than they were while working at the physical office location. One of the managers, William, said to me over a zoom call, 'Payal, I've never worked as hard my whole life as I am during this lockdown. I'd never imagined that work-from-home would be so much more hectic than work-from-workplace. I've been putting in 19-20 hours a day.' My immediate question to him was, 'if you are so frustrated with the situation, have you spoken to your boss or your team about it?' He looked at me and said, 'oh no, Payal, I wouldn't do that. What if I come across as lazy, uncommitted, or not a team player. I sure want to protect my image as a hard worker.'

DOI: 10.4324/9781003260714-5

After a couple of months, I met William again at a virtual conference I was speaking at. After the conference, he reached out to me separately over a call and said, 'Payal, I work so hard. I do more than I should, and yet guess what? My boss doesn't value me. She keeps adding work to my schedule. I find it ridiculous.' William ended his statement with a disappointed look. I looked at William and adjusted my headphones, saying,

> Of course she values you, William. By working hard and taking more and more on yourself, she knows your value and keeps adding more work on your agenda because she is sure you will not only take up the work but also deliver it.

'Oh, is that so?' William asked with a confusing look.

'OK, so what do I do now? How do I go and tell her about how I feel?' 'You don't,' I said immediately. 'Listen to me, William,' I said, going right into the screen. 'No one needs to go to people and tell them that they need to be valued or respected or treated in a certain way. The only thing you and any of us must do is to be authentic.' There was silence from the other side. For a moment, I thought I had lost William due to network issues. But he was there, reflecting on what I said. He told me that he has decided to sign up for my executive coaching session to be a better leader. A transformed leader because he wanted to win the leadership game.

Each of us at our workplaces has in some way experienced the feeling of being undervalued or disrespected or treated in ways that we disapprove of. And when this happens, what do we do? We get angry from the inside and share our grievances with everyone around, except with the person we should share. We often behave as if everything is fine, and we move on, signaling that we are all good. We put up a 'leadership act.' It continues to surprise me how many leaders act one way at work while their 'true' personality emerges outside of work. And it surprises me, even more to see these leaders shocked and confused when their employees don't trust them and can't relate to them. If only we are authentic enough.

This is why I urge leaders to practice the law of authenticity, which fundamentally means that you are your true self. It's about knowing who you are, being who you are, and showing your authentic self. It's a state where you feel free, easy, calm, undisturbed, untroubled, centered, and peaceful. When you are your authentic self, you operate in a state of bliss. The desire to live authentically is an innate drive within each of us. The self that we indeed are is always seeking to manifest itself ever more fully. How many times have you said to yourself or heard someone say that 'I just want to be myself.' We say this because we have many selves. We have a social self, a professional self, and a private self. As a leader, you need to know which self is appropriate in a given situation. Your main job is to recognize your authentic self-detached from all other-selves of you. No project is more valuable than finding your true self. When people don't know their authentic selves, they give in to desires or say yes when they want to say no.

As Aristotle said, knowing yourself is the beginning of all wisdom. You've got to be familiar with your values and with your most dominant thoughts to know yourself. To find your authentic self, all you need to do is answer this simple question: What would you like to do if there were no consequences for any of your actions? What would you like to do if there wasn't anyone around to look at you, judge you, punish you, or even know about what you did?

What would you like to do if you had the power to do anything in this world, or rather this universe?

## THE MONK WHO STAYED TRUE TO HIS NATURE

*I remember a story I once read about a Monk walking alongside a stream when he saw a Scorpion struggling in the water. Knowing that Scorpions cannot swim, he quickly plunged into the water to rescue it.*

*Carefully, he picked the Scorpion up with his fingers and walked to the bank. Just when he was about to set the Scorpion down, it turned and stung his hand. The Monk being in pain, drew his hand back, and as a result, the Scorpion was flung back into the stream.*

*When the Monk realized what happened, he went back into the water and picked up the Scorpion again. Just as the Monk was about to set the Scorpion down, he was again stung on the hand by it, but he finally saved the Scorpion. A little boy was playing by the stream when he witnessed this whole incident. Being confused, he asked the Monk, 'Excuse me. Why do you keep trying to save that Scorpion? It stings you every time you try to rescue it.'*

*The Monk replied, 'Dear boy, just as it is the water's nature to make me wet, so it is the nature of the Scorpion to sting. And just as it is the Scorpion's nature to sting, it is my nature to save.'*

I found this a meaningful tale that tells us that we should not change our behaviors or thoughts based on the behaviors or opinions of others. We may come across those who harm and insult us due to their ignorance or lack of understanding, but we must never allow their actions to rob us of our duties and faith. It's one thing to improve your nature and find better ways to apply it, and it's another thing to be foolish and continue with a nature of quality that can harm you and others around it.

The Buddha taught that your true nature is emptiness, and when this true nature is realized, the divine states of loving-kindness, compassion, empathetic joy, and equanimity emerge. Your authentic self is not dependant on anyone else. Your authentic self is happy, cheerful, and peaceful. But we allow the external events to disturb our authentic self, and negativity, unhappiness, and a turbulent mind dominate our behavior. And then, we begin to believe that we must look outside for happiness, peace, and joy. We forget that these are our true nature that is buried deep down in us.

To be your authentic self, you must locate your north star—your true purpose—and incorporate it into your life. Too often, we don't realize what we truly want or have trouble defining exactly what inspires us and what is missing from our lives. It is our unidentified limiting beliefs and behaviors that prevent us from being authentic.

I once came across an article in the New York Times about how Germany has renamed a military base to honor a World War II Army sergeant. This particular sergeant, Anton Schmid, an Austrian serving in the German army, saved more than 250 Jews from extermination. He disobeyed his superior officers and helped these men, women, and children escape by hiding them and supplying them with false identification papers. The Nazis executed Sergeant Schmid for his acts.

Sergeant Schmid's actions reveal the wonderment and pain of what it means to realize one's true nature.

## THE WIDESPREAD AASD SYNDROME

Being your authentic self can feel risky now in our screen-obsessed world. We're just trying to fit in, be liked, and be accepted by other human beings.

Some years back, I was invited to my client's annual corporate gathering in Nepal. While there, I got an opportunity to engage with some of the top executives from the banking industry. I remember this one senior vice president with whom I may have engaged in an excellent conversation for at least half an hour. While taking my leave, he asked me a question that made me think about how dependent we are on other people's views about us.

He asked me, 'Payal, what type of a person do I come across? Am I a leader whom people would love to follow, or am I someone people would ignore?' At that moment, I told him the truth that he was a remarkable person whom anyone could relate to.

Later that night, I thought about his question and wondered, what if I had been his colleagues and someone jealous of his personality and growth and just said that he comes across as a negative person whose team might ignore him? You see, many people criticize you for destroying you from within. There is a difference between constructive feedback and destructive criticism.

His question reminded me of millions of people who suffer from what I call the AASD syndrome. And this disease hits everyone from the individual contributors and travels upward to the highest management level. I've met super successful entrepreneurs who suffer from AASD Syndrome and I've met managers who go through AASD. So what is AASD? It's an acronym for Approval and Attention Seeking Disorder. It's very prevalent at workplaces. It's a disorder where you try hard to make others happy at the cost of you. It's the biggest reason why we don't see authenticity at our workplace. People with AASD will often go out of their way to please someone, even if it means taking valuable time or resources away from themselves. For instance, has it ever happened to you that your boss comes up to your desk and says, let's do our 1:1 meeting over lunch today? How about a sandwich lunch? And you respond saying, 'Ya sure. I love sandwiches.' Whereas in reality, you hate sandwiches. Now, this may sound like a seemingly small instance, and you might be saying to yourself, it's OK, not a big deal. But guess what, it's these everyday small instances where you shrink your opinion that slowly gets into your DNA, and before you even know it, you've caught the AASD. And by the time you realize it, it's become chronic.

Here are some symptoms of Approval and Attention Seeking Disorder

1. You say yes to people when you want to say no.
2. You feel it's important to be liked by everyone.
3. You often do too much for people, so you are liked.
4. You go to great lengths to avoid conflicts.
5. You have a low opinion of yourself.
6. You apologize or accept fault when you aren't to blame.
7. You're quick to agree, even when you don't agree.
8. You feel responsible for how other people feel.
9. You avoid making decisions or sharing your opinions.
10. You break your values for others and regret them later.

Do any of these relate to you? I encourage you to identify from the above list if you have AASD and at what level. Is it at the beginning stage, or is it chronic?

You see, to win the leadership game, you've got to be your authentic self. And being a people pleaser isn't true to yourself. Most of us don't bring our authentic selves to work, mainly because we get into people-pleasing behavior. Being a people pleaser and suffering from the AASD Syndrome takes a toll on your mental and physical well-being. I was coaching a CEO of a midsize retail firm. He had a hard time letting his people know when their ideas and plans weren't on track. So when he hired me for a speed coaching session (these are my special coachings sessions that help solve an immediately pressing problem), I gauged that he was uncomfortable being straightforward to his team. He cared too much about being an encouraging and supportive boss. So knowing that it would be tough for him to give up immediately on this habit, I encouraged him to ask questions. Then whenever his team would bring on some ideas or plans, he would ask them questions like—'how will it generate the results we are targeting?' or 'Do we have the required support and budget?' Slowly he moved from being a people pleaser to a people's leader.

People who aren't authentic don't make great leaders, can't spark fantastic conversation, and constantly feel overextended. And many times, we aren't our authentic selves because we want to feel a sense of job security in these unprecedented business times like Julia, whom I met at a friend's home, and we connected well. I got to know she worked at a large IT company as a manager. Julia had worked hard for this position. During our friendship, I got to know so much more about Julia. She was selfless and often took up a lot of work on herself. She gladly accepted any piece of work her boss gave her. She offered to work on presentations that her colleague was stuck on. People would often compliment her on her selfless nature and tell her how happy they felt to have her around. Soon, without realizing it, Julia got into the habit of making everyone around her happy. But she also began feeling stressed and burnt out at work. She began to keep her head down, work hard, and keep everyone at work comfortable. Let me tell you, Julai was a great product developer. She was full of incredible ideas, but when asked by her boss for suggestions, she would not say anything because she feared displeasing her bosses. Finally, during the recession in America, her company was forced to downsize, and Julia's name topped the list.

What was the cause of Julia's downfall? She was focused on pleasing others and gaining approval that she forgot her authentic self. Most of us don't even realize how and when we slip into destructive behaviors. We think that being kind, gentle, and agreeable guarantees us to win love, respect, and acceptance from others. It's just the opposite. The more you please people, the more you get treated like an old dishrag, ultimately disliking yourself. A people pleaser is worried about rejection. There are many causes of people-pleasing behavior, and they start with the belief we hold about ourselves in relation to others. People pleasing can undermine your ability to lead effectively. Leaders who try too hard to be nice soon begin to feel pressured to be nice, and then they come across as lacking integrity. They avoid confrontation. They avoid conflicts and challenging situations.

You may think that being a people-pleaser serves you well at work. However, as a leader, this trait will ultimately fail you. It will stop you from expressing your actual needs, wants and opinions, and will cause you to make some bad choices. It also makes leading people a challenge because you will be operating in a state of excessive worry, rumination, and frustration. In turn, this leads to stress and panic. Every decision a leader makes is subject to opinion. Most of us who have leadership positions want people to like us personally and in our role as a leader. We all like to be appreciated, and this often leads us to become victims of people pleasing. When you aim to please people, you are often motivated more by what people want than what the organization wants. It is dangerous. Leaders who suffer from AASD are people pleasers who often witness tension in the team, burnout, disloyalty, and mediocrity. Being a people-pleaser undermines your leadership.

I know that no one sets out to be a people pleaser. We want to be our authentic selves at work. What stops us is our culture and the need to be liked. I grew up in a very happy family. Such a happy family that when I got my first leadership role, I thought it was my duty to keep everyone happy. That conflict is terrible and must be avoided. That I must put everyone's needs before mine, and guess what? I failed miserably at my job then. In the years to come, doing a lot of work and research on people skills, I learned that people pleasers often act the way they do because of their insecurities and lack of self-esteem. So if I was trying to keep everyone in my team happy, the underlying cause was the insecurity of not being a likable leader.

Think about people you know in your team and workplace. Can you think of anyone who suffers from AASD? Are you battling AASD? It's nothing to shy away with. AASD is something to face and get cured of so that you can move faster on your path to success. Once you are free from this disease, you can connect better with people, you move faster toward your goal, you will create an identity for yourself, you will find out who your real friends and supporters are, you will be more productive, and you will free up a lot more time.

Now, it's not that you must go about saying a strict no to everyone and everything around you. It doesn't mean you shouldn't care about others' needs and choices. It's not about being selfish. But don't be a person who, when asked what kind of food you enjoy or which restaurant you'd like to dine at, quickly says, 'whatever you want is fine.' Don't be a colleague who cheerfully volunteers to do the lion's share of work but later backbites unexpectedly or reports to the project manager about the work pressure? What I've learned in my two decades of work is that you don't want to be a person who, regardless of how it will inconvenience you, will bend over backward to get others what they need.

Don't be afraid to disagree with your colleagues when you feel they are about to cross that line. Stand up for your position. As Steve Jobs rightly said—'If you want to make everyone happy, don't be a leader—Sell Ice Cream.' It's something I reminded my daughter constantly when I saw her getting onto the track of wanting to make everyone around her happy at the cost of her own time and work. Remember, when you say NO to someone or something, you are saying YES to yourself—to your dreams and your life. You are being true to yourself.

## THE TRANSITION FROM PEOPLE PLEASER TO PEOPLE LEADER

The number one rule to becoming more authentic is to stop being a people pleaser. Leadership is not about keeping your team happy; it is about making them feel valuable, respected, engaged, and energized. How do you do that? How do you build a high-performing team of resilient people who don't need to be constantly pleased by the world around them? How do you make lasting connections with people without being a people pleaser? By following a couple of simple practices called ASAP. Here's what ASAP reflects:

**Aspire:** One of the key expectations from any leader is providing a vision. Setting significant, compelling, or even nearly impossible goals allows you to be engaged and motivated in the long run and also gives our team a purpose. You need to state where the organization is heading and outline steps on how you expect that it gets there. This way, you will know when to whom and what you can say a yes. You will be able to set your priorities. When you try to please all kinds of people, you usually end up sacrificing your aspirations. And I am sure you don't want that. So keep your aspirations high as these will guide you to be authentic. It is easy to say yes to every request on your time when your life priorities are unclear. When your days are not guided by a rich and inspiring vision for your future, a clear image of a result that will help you act more intentionally, it is not hard for the agendas of those around you to dictate your actions. In my 21 years of coaching people to be great leaders, I've noticed how unclear they are about their vision and goals.

**Self-upliftment:** My father once gave me this advice which has helped me a lot in my life. He said, 'Payal, nobody can give you wiser advice than yourself. So at all times, keep uplifting yourself so that you give great advice yourself.' He couldn't have been more right. Out of everyone you know in the world, the only person that is always omni present in your life, non-negotiable, day and night, is you. So from time to time, you need to work on yourself. When we have a harmonic relationship with ourselves, we no longer look to other people to fill gaps in our life. As Wayne Dyer said, 'You can never feel lonely when you like the person you're alone with.' 'When you indulge in self-doubt, self-pity, self-criticism, and other such limiting thoughts and behaviors, your contract the AASD. When you decide to correct the course on your way to success and indulge in self-upliftment, you become a people leader.'

**Abandon:** I have noticed that successful people can focus on what makes the most significant difference. It requires saying no to a lot of things that might be urgent but not important. When you say no, you begin to master the art of time management and decision-making—both of which are necessary to boost your leadership. So here are ten things you must start saying NO to accelerate your growth and progress.

1. Say no to other people's emotional baggage.
2. Say no to the friend who wants to meet over coffee to gossip.
3. Say no to the coworker who wants to spread his negativity and cynicism.
4. Say no to the people who laugh at your dreams.
5. Say no to people who make you doubt yourself.
6. Say no to projects that aren't aligned with your dream.
7. Say no to the social obligations that drain time from your life's work.
8. Say no to average so you can say yes to the awesomeness.
9. Say no to laziness and unhealthy foods.
10. Say no to being perfect so you can say YES to mistakes.

Here's a bonus one

11. Say no to people who use you for their advantage.

**Procrastinate:** Once, while I was delivering my high-impact master class 'The Unstoppable Leader' at a Fortune 100 company in London, I had someone from the audience ask me, 'Payal, How do I say a direct no to my boss? I could lose my job.' I agree. It's tough to say no to your boss's request; it's even harder when you are a people pleaser. But there are ways to tell a no, which makes you look professional and a thought leader. So the next time you have a boss or a colleague asking you to be a part of their project, rather than saying an immediate 'OK' and regretting later, say something like this: 'Thanks for asking me. Sounds interesting. Let me think and get back to you on this.' Now this shows you are not in a hurry just to grab any project that comes your way. It showcases you as a mindful person who knows your goal. It gives you some space to think about it and respond on email or text with a polite 'no' or a 'yes.' But the decision is well thought of. And this response takes only a millisecond but gives you ample time.

Often I found it extremely difficult to say *no* only because I didn't know how to express myself with clarity and confidence, fearing I could sound aggressive or impolite. I learned to say no with grace, without offending anyone.

Here are some simple formulas that always work well for me:

- It doesn't work for me right now.
- I'm not able to make it this Sunday/this week/month/year.
- I've got too much on my plate right now.
- Thank you for thinking of me; I'm sorry I can't at this time.
- It's too bad I'm busy, but please let me know how it turns out.
- Perhaps another time; let me know what next week looks like for you.

*As Paulo Coelho rightly said, 'When you say Yes to others, make sure you are not saying no to yourself.'* If someone asks for a favor, take time to think about it and check your schedule. Don't let your mouth say 'Yes' before your brain has time to give the request thoughtful consideration.

So here's some work for you—I want you to make a list of things you must say no to focus on yourself and impact your career. This time, don't make a to-do list. Instead, make a not-to-list—maybe they are people, assignments, or habits that you've got to say no to. Do this and see the difference.

We all have been given the same 24 hours in the day. Be wise and use the word NO often; as I had written in my book Success Is Within, if your priorities don't get scheduled into your planner, other people's priorities will get put into your planner. Be the owner of your time and calendar. Imagine how great your life will be when you own your time.

We all want to be authentic—but we also want to fit in. Practicing authenticity consistently can be challenging, but by refusing to hide your honest opinions and needs, you'll be your authentic self every day. To become a world-class leader, you need to realize that you can't be all things to all people. It's essential for you to be consciously aware of your priorities, goals, and your dreams and for you to feel that you played your best game as a human being. Sure, some people around you will not be happy with your NO. But would you rather live your life according to the approval of others or aligned with your truth and your dreams?

## RAPID ACTION PLAN (RAP)

Take some time and reflect on this question—what will you do today to transition from AASD to ASAP?

# 4

## Law of Circle

While the economy transitions into a completely digital one because of Covid-19, I am often asked this question—'Payal, what is the way to succeed in these challenging times?' And I answer it by saying—build your circle. And the immediate response is, 'Oh, I see, so it's all about networking.' 'No, not really,' I say. Think about how many network events you have been to. What about times when you felt awkward going to a networking event or procrastinated? I am sure those times are plenty on your list. And what did you do at these events? Meet and greet unknown faces, put on a plastic smile even after an exhausting day at work, talk about yourself, exchange cards, engage in forced interactions, have dinner, and then go back home. What's the most you ever got out of these events? A couple of business cards which you didn't use? A few more LinkedIn connections than you had the day before?

How often have you attended a business trade show or a general networking event and come back to the office and said that it was a complete waste of your time? Trust me when I say IBT—I've been there.

In the year 2000, when I relocated to the United States, I was utterly lost. I didn't know anyone in this country then. No family, no uncle, and aunts and friends either. It was just my husband and me in a new country, halfway across the world. Finally, after some struggle, I got a job as an HR generalist. And slowly, I began to connect with people within my organization. I met people in the cafeteria, exchanged emails, and built some valuable connections. In 2002, after one and half years of my job, the dot com industry crashed, leading to a significant economic recession and unemployment. My name was among the people laid off in my company. But this time, I felt confident enough because I had built a network of some valuable connections. I reached out to them, called them, and emailed

DOI: 10.4324/9781003260714-6

some. Most of them did not respond, and a few only responded, sympathizing with my situation. And here I was, sitting on my work desk in my two-bedroom apartment (in those days, I did not own a million-dollar home as I do now), surrounded by all the business cards I had accumulated through my network. Things looked grim for a while before I landed my next job; I thought of playing it smarter this time. Rather than only networking inside my organization, I took the time and effort to cross the network at various conferences, meetup groups, associations, and events. I was able to reach out to more people. I was happy with my progress. Down the line, I observed that out of hundreds of contacts I built, only a couple of them truly matter. Whatever happened to the others, I wondered? So much effort, time, and money went for just a couple of people to respond and stay connected with you. I began feeling disheartened. For some years, I gave up on the idea of networking. I continued with my job, gave my best, and worked hard. Then after three years of working tirelessly for the company, there came up an internal opening for a project manager. My credentials and work profile exactly matched the job opening, and my colleagues encouraged me to apply. I did. I got rejected. They gave the offer to another person named Kyle from the same department. I was disheartened. I blamed discrimination because it was a male colleague who got the role who had the same credentials and worked profile as mine.

Everything for me changed in the year 2007. I clearly remember the evening of December of 2007, when the CEO of this mid-size company I was working for addressed the leadership team for 15 minutes during the companies' all-hand leadership event. Some of the best relationship-building advice I learned from his speech was that one must intentionally develop their inner circle. And that your potential is determined by those closest to you.

After a few months, I learned that Kyle, who was promoted over me, was the person who barely went to network events or after office networking. But he had built a tight inner circle up, down, across the organization, and outside. Because of this, opportunities landed in his lap every time. Whatever be the economy, it's all about your circle.

The Law of the circle is simple. It says that you cannot do it alone. This Law is based on the fact of the universe that states that everything and every person is somehow connected to each other. The connection is omnipresent. We have to be observant and tune into it. You need a group of people with whom you get along and who are your 'go-to's' for sound advice, inspiration, ideas, creative stimulation, and truth. As Mother Teresa said, 'You can do what I can't do. I can do what you can't do. Together we can do great things.' That is the power of the Law of the Circle.

Every leader's potential is determined by the people closest to them. If those people are strong, then the leader can make a huge impact. If they are weak, they can't. It's a small group of people who will never let you fail. They are your lifelines. It's a group of people who advise you when you need it the most. Your circle is a support network made up of people who will give you the encouragement, advice, and guidance you need in your professional life. People who have your back when you most need it. It's an intentional process where you consciously pick great friends, mentors, peers, co-workers, and partners who can push you when you need a boost and provide a platform to generate breakthrough ideas. If you do not have a strong circle, I cannot recommend highly enough that you go about thinking and building one today. Have you surrounded yourself with a circle of strong leaders?

## THE STORY IS WRONG

Our culture loves the idea of the genius leader who accomplishes everything on their own. That self-made man or woman idol is what we've been wrongly shown. We want to believe that Steve Jobs created all of his Apple products by himself in his parents' garage. Or Nelson Mandela single-handedly freed South Africa from Apartheid.

We read stories of rags to riches and top successful leaders, assuming they just had it in them. Here's the truth, my friend, none of us do anything significant all by ourselves. If you do, well, that's sad because you will not only end up burnt out but also will be incredibly lonely. Maybe this is why they say it's lonely at the top. No one succeeds alone. No one fails alone. Besides your luck and hard work, your success and failure have a lot to do with your inner circle.

An article in CNBC said that when Indra Nooyi first took the reins as PepsiCo's CEO in 2006, she reached out to tech titan Steve Jobs. She wanted his insight on how he ran and transformed Apple. The lessons he shared with her were 'phenomenal,' she said, and she implemented many throughout her tenure as PepsiCo's chief executive.

The most ancient business wisdom goes like this: connections solve everything. A wise person once noted that the time to build your circle is not when you *need* a network but as soon as you enter the workforce, even while you are in your undergrad. I remember teaching my daughters the importance of their circle right from when they were in high school. They began keeping up with a few of their teachers and principals, along with their mentors and internship employers. It eventually helped them a long way in their careers.

As you progress in your life and career, you will meet hundreds of people. Everyone will have something in common with you, and some might be just the opposite of who you are. You create and decide your circle.

There are two primary layers of your circle which I ask people to build in their career lives: the macro layer and the microlayer. The Marco layer includes mentors, close colleagues, team members and extends anywhere from ten people in your circle to a hundred. This is called the inner circle.

Then there is the microlayer, which is your tight winner circle. There are roughly five to ten people in your life with whom you share an intimate connection and lifelong closeness. Keeping them close means staying in touch with them regularly and ensuring your relationships are high-caliber. You'll likely keep an eye on that quality-over-time tracker to make sure things remain strong. And there will always be movement at both these levels. Some will come inside your circles, and some will leave. Movement is good. Else your circle will be stagnant, and that is the worst for winning.

The winner's circle is rare to find and some of the world's top executives build it for themselves.

It's in this area that most people feel challenged. It's an area that most leaders find difficult to accomplish. You must be a master in developing your winner circle to win the leadership game.

## YOU NEED A WINNER'S CIRCLE

In June of 2020, I received an email from one of the CEO's consultants I am closely associated with. Before the virus, she spent 90% of her time traveling and consulting top CEOs. The pandemic changed everything. It impacted the work from which she made a significant living. Her company began downsizing and closing down some departments. In October 2020, the company offered to take the CEO package and step down as the company could no longer afford her services. Rather than hiding her face in the sand or living in anxiety, or blaming the economy, she shifted and adapted. She set up her consultancy firm to help women reach the C-suite positions and created a networking group. And guess who supported her and advised her? Yes, her winner circle, the microlayer people.

Do you have a winner's circle? Who do you look to for sage advice? So, where do you find the support you need? We all need people who will listen to us, bounce around ideas, or offer a valued opinion. We need a winner's circle. A group of people we can count on in good times and bad. Those people will make a massive contribution to our success.

In our life, most of us come up against personal and professional problems that are just too big to solve alone. If we want to be as successful as we know we can be, we need the help of others. We need the advice and support of people we trust.

Building a winner circle is very different from an inner circle or any other circle or networking group. When it comes to networks or social circles, the bigger, the better. Networking groups are your macro layer.

But when it comes to building your winner circle, the microlevel, the tighter, the better. Most people think of the winner circle as something to be made when you reach way up high on the corporate ladder. At the same time, others link it to playing dirty corporate politics. While it may be true, it's not always the case. Your winner circle is your cheerleaders most of the time if you have been cautious while choosing them. The responsibilities of owning a business or leading a team are substantial, from making the right choices when strategically planning to hiring and firing when building a team. It can be overwhelming at times. Particularly when we face challenges, sometimes they seem to hit us one after another. Who's in your winner circle? The best way to grow as a leader is to have a mixture of people in your winner circle.

Take some time in solitude and think of people who you have or want in your inner circle and in your winner's circle. Are there people who should be in these circles but aren't? Are there people who are in these circles but shouldn't be?

When it comes to growth and success, we are greatly influenced by those closest to us—whether we like it or not. It affects our way of thinking, our self-esteem, and our decisions.

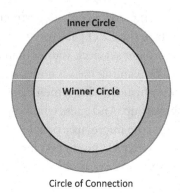

Circle of Connection

**FIGURE 4.1**
Circle of Connection

## HOW TO CREATE A WINNER'S CIRCLE

The inner circle is famous in the corporate world. People build their inner circle while trying to get into an influencer's inner circle or based on their network group. This tradition has been going on for decades in the business world. An inner circle works based on who knows who and what they can do for me. It's about corporate politics, and everyone comes in with their private agenda, most of which is to grow through the ranks.

But a winner's circle is very different.

Imagine you spend your whole life in one room and that one room has only one door. That one door is the only door. So when people come in, they are there forever, and you can never get them out. If this were real and not a metaphor, wouldn't you be more selective on who you let into your life? To make better decisions on who you let into your room, you need to know your values. Do you have deal breakers for what is unacceptable to have in a personal or professional relationship? Knowing this will help you to understand what your values are.

Once on a flight from Atlanta to Raleigh, I met Stephen, CEO of the agricultural industry. We spoke of business and general stuff and found some commonality between us when it came to leadership. Later as we built more of our relationship, I learned he was a man of powerful influence and could connect me to many in business. Our talks and advice continued over some time, and we built a good rapport. Once, he asked if

I could do a couple of complimentary sessions for his team as the agriculture sector is run on government funds, and they don't have a budget for training and development. I found myself in a dilemma. If I would oblige, it means I would need to oblige to Someone Someone else from my inner circle, too if they would have a similar request. If I decline, I could lose him from my inner circle. It was a tough decision to make. My husband told me that if it's just one or two sessions of an hour each, there is no harm doing it. At least he will stay connected with you, and that I shouldn't forget he is highly influential. My mind, heart, and soul weren't getting aligned to go forward with this request.

So here's what I did. I took the time to write a handwritten letter to him explaining my beliefs and the values by which I live and do my work. I demonstrated my work ethic and how it would be hard to weave in his request because accepting it would be unfair to my other clients and associates, who I might decline for a similar request. I sent the letter with a beautiful Indian handicraft token.

But, let me tell you, I had not even the slightest idea of what the consequence of this would be. Maybe he wouldn't reply at all, or perhaps he would respond with his discontent, or maybe he would support my values. I did not hear back from him for two months. Then one Saturday afternoon, I had a courier person deliver to my doorstep this beautiful acrylic painting with my name and symbol of a growing relationship. The gift was from Stephen. And since then, we have bonded more than before.

What are your values? How would you define your values? Values are fundamental beliefs that guide or motivate attitudes or actions. They help us to determine what is important to us. They provide the general guidelines for conduct. They highlight what we stand for. Leadership occurs within the context of core values. Values can have a significant impact on your winning the leadership game. Core values determine how you execute administration, create your team environment, and be in the room with you.

Knowing your values and what you stand for will help you to build the right inner circle and take the right actions. When you know and stand for your values, your inner circle will most likely be of people who have similar values and who stand for them. A winner's circle is based more on values than on personal agenda.

It goes beyond personal agendas and corporate politics.

Let your room of winner circle be filled with some of these people:

- Learner: The friend who asks, 'Hey, you want to do this visioning workshop together?' is the friend who is saying she wants you to grow.
- Cheerleader: This is the person who celebrates the progress, not just the outcome; the person who knows how hard you worked on something.
- Dreamers think of things that others do not. They help you imagine *what if*.
- Driver: The driver brings the dream to reality.
- Motivator: This is your voice of inspiration that keeps pushing you to meet your goals.
- Sponsor: Someone in a real position to guide and influence your progress through the maze and politics of advancement.

Who we surround ourselves with determines our level of success, happiness, fulfillment, joy, gratitude, and performance. The right circle of influence raises the bar, helping us to set new, loftier expectations of ourselves. Often we don't know what we are capable of until we see others achieve.

You won't build the winner's circle overnight. It takes time, shared experiences, and shared values to develop meaningful relationships—just like you and your best friend didn't become besties overnight. Most people fail to make investments in meaningful relationships, and they pay the price in mediocrity. Your potential as a leader relies on the quality of people in your inner circle.

---

## WHO'S AT THE CORE OF THE WINNER'S CIRCLE

My older daughter often catches me speaking to myself in whispers and questions me, 'hey mon, who's with you? Who are you even talking with?' And I just brush it off lightly, saying to her, 'if you see me talking to myself, please go your way. I am self-employed, and we are having a staff meeting.'

But here's the truth, when you become your own best friend, life is much simpler. Leaders are around people the majority of the time. Being strategic about your winner circle means you take your time to determine who and how many people will be in your process. And while you build your inner circle, the first person to add to this tight group is YOU. This is the person who will always be available to give you advice. That's what William, a workaholic CEO of a struggling but still viable start-up, did not do.

On one Sunday evening, while he was at his office desk, scrolling through his email, an email message from his company's Vice President, Ava, popped up with the subject—'Sorry.' William opened it and was stunned at what it read—'Hard decision...feel terrible leaving you at this crucial time...' William scrolled up and down, and read the detailed message containing the explanation of her decision. He tried to reach Ava, but she did not respond to his calls. Finally, after three hours, she took his call. She admitted she had an irresistible offer from a company she had wanted to work with for years. William tried to convince her to stay, offering the best package he could. But Ava had made up her mind. She wanted to advance in her career. Ava was the only person in Williams' team of five people who could scale the business. And now she is gone.

That evening William wanted to talk to someone, someone. He thought of all the people in his tight inner circle, from an old friend and a venture capitalist to his wife and confidant to his network. But no one was available. William spent the rest of the night and the next two days horribly. If only William had added his name to that list, he would be able to sit with himself and think through this too.

It's necessary to add yourself to the list of your winner circle. Let your name be in the center of the list. Because when you reach out to your winner circle during the most crucial time of your life, let me warn you, there will be times when no one from it is available to you. And if you haven't trained yourself well enough to be the core of this circle, you will feel low, frustrated, and lack clarity.

When you truly realize that you can depend on yourself, there isn't a river you can't cross or a problem you can't think your way out of. If there is one thing you will learn, the hard way or the easy way, when all is said and done, the only person you can trust is yourself. Everyone has different motives, and no matter how close they are to you, they will disappear as fast as they came in when you need them most.

There will be points in your life where you hit rock bottom and feel alone, but instead of losing your mind and thinking you are worthless, you need to take that time to understand the only person you have: yourself. So keep yourself at the center of your inner circle.

Now, when it comes to the winner circle, there are two dimensions to it. One is getting into the winner's circle of top management at your workplace. The other is building your winner circle. Both are imperative for your organic growth.

While doing a 1:1 coaching session with a senior manager from CISCO, he asked me this question—Payal, I want to get into my vice president's inner circle. But the harder I try, the more difficult it gets. How can I get into his inner circle? Breaking into the CEO's or your top management's inner circle requires more than just sending emails or pitching in the elevator.

It requires actions like the one taken by Divya. Divya joined as a technical assistant in a mid-sized IT firm in San Jose. After six months of working at the company, she sent a handwritten letter to the company chairman stating that she feels she isn't being fully utilized for her talents and is overpaid compared to the work she is given. The following day she received a call. They spoke for 15 minutes, and based on her abilities and skills, he suggested she take up some vital company projects. From then on, there have been frequent interactions between them about work and ideas. Within seven months, Divya, who works as a project manager, is a part of his inner circle, working with some of the top management in the company.

Mathew had recently graduated from an engineering college and was looking for a job in yet another instance. He was great at programing to block hackers. He somehow managed to get a 2-minute appointment with the CEO. Mathew began explaining his program but failed to convince the CEO of its benefits. After almost a year and a half after this incident, Mathew read in the news that this same bank's site got hacked. Mathew immediately went to their corporate office. He said to the receptionist that he knew how to block hackers immediately and create a program that would track them down. He gets an entry to meet the CEO, who is in a meeting with the bank's top officials discussing the hacking that took place. Within a hundred seconds, he stopped the hacking as well as got the hackers traced. The CEO of the company gave him the work to build software that prevents hackers. He has been in the CEO's inner circle since then.

In my case, at the age of 23 years, while in my role as an HR lead in the Copper Chimney chain of restaurants, due to my successful work of removing unions from the company, the then-chairperson of the company called me into his office for coffee. As nervous as I was, I faked up my confidence while sitting opposite him at his office. He praised me for my work and introduced me to some huge names in the restaurant business who were facing similar union problems. From then on, I was in his inner circle.

I think by now you've got my point. Your position, age, job description, status quo, gender, or title does not decide who is in your inner circle and whose inner circle you are in. Your work fixes it.

So the next time you are wondering how to get into the winner circle of top management, ask yourself this question, 'What value am I providing to their inner circle?'

So carefully curate your most trusted inner circle, and you'll be surprised at how much more valuable you'll become to the larger community of people in the world who care about the same things you do.

Do you want to be a winner at leadership? Make sure you do not break the Law of the circle.

## RAPID ACTION PLAN

Make a list of people you want in your winner's circle. Make a list of people in whose winner's circle you are?

# 5

## Law of Problems

There is a common thread between you, me, and every human being on this planet earth, and the thread is of problems.

My father often quotes, 'every human being has one thing in common problems. No one on this planet earth is free of problems. It's only the degree of the problem that varies.' Now I know it's tempting to think that the rich and famous have so much money, what problem could they possibly have? They look so happy and prosperous. Although they might not be having issues with their finances, they are struggling with other problems that we don't know about. Everyone is constantly working with something: your boss, your colleagues, your clients, and your team. Everyone has a problem; only the degree varies. And add to this that every person on this planet earth also seeks happiness. Once you understand this deep element, you can connect with people of any personality. When you see people, remember this equation that people are made of problems and happiness. Everyone has their share of trials and joy.

People = Problems + Happiness

The Law of Problem is based on the above equation, which says that your job as a master connector is to connect with people's problems and help them reduce them or connect with their happiness (what makes them happy) and help them increase it. Honestly, it's easier to connect with people's problems because most of us overlook the amount of happiness we already have in our lives. We are inclined to focus more on our problems and have a deep desire to eliminate them. Of these two, we're wired to work harder to avoid pain.

Look at your work life. You will see you have a hundred reasons to be happy and passionate about your work and just a couple of reasons to be

DOI: 10.4324/9781003260714-7

unhappy. Yet, you will notice how much time you spend on the negative aspects of your work.

Another interesting thing here is that most of us feel our problems are more significant than anyone else on this earth. Often people share with me the problems they have at their workplace, and I tell them to look around, and they will see millions of people who would happily take up your situation just to get one job.

In a few of my corporate masterclasses, I play a simple game with my audience. Each of them is given a sticky note and asked to name their top three problems without mentioning their name. Then I pass out a large bowl and invite people to fold their post-it note and drop it in the bowl. I shuffle it and ask everyone to take out one post-it note from the bowl and read the problem written in it. Then I asked the audience to raise their hand if anyone would be willing to trade their problem with what they have in the note. No one has ever raised their hand and said, 'yes, I would like to exchange my problem.' People are surprised that specific problems which they were never aware of exist in someone's life. But everyone realizes the main aim of this game is that no one in that room is free of problems.

The Law of Problem is based on the universal truth that everyone has pain points, and everyone wants to reduce or get away with their problems. Whether or not there is rainfall, there are always problems in life. Everybody has problems.

Whatever you think is going wrong, whatever problems you think you have, someone always has it worse. I promise you. There are people without jobs, people fighting aggressive illnesses in hospitals, people with businesses going bankrupt.

To win the leadership game, connecting with people's problems is of utmost importance. Your job is to connect not with people and their work. Your main job is to connect with people's problems. And in doing so, not only will you win over them and forget your problems, but also you will make them your lifelong connection. That's how salespeople and advertisements focus on the problems and fears that you carry. If I were to ask you to list your problems and blessings, I could almost bet your list of problems will surpass your list of blessings simply because we humans are wired to think more about our problems.

# FIND THE NICHE

I remember reading an article about Dr. Kalam, an Indian aerospace scientist who served as the 11th President of India from 2002 to 2007. During a hectic project, one of the 70 scientists working on it asked Dr. Kalam if he could leave at 5.30 pm that evening as he had promised to take his kids to an exhibition. Dr. Kalam permitted him. However, the scientist got busy with work only to realize that it was 8.30 pm. When he looked for his boss, he wasn't there. Guilty for having disappointed his kids, he went home only to find that his kids weren't there. When he asked his wife where they were, she replied, 'You don't know? Your manager came here at 5.15 pm and took the children to the exhibition.'

When Dr. Kalam noticed him working hard at 5 pm, he thought that this person would not leave work, but they would enjoy the exhibition if he had promised his children. So he, the boss, took the lead. Dr. Kalam knew that his scientist's problem was between completing the job and leaving on time for the kids. He connected with that problem and added value.

Jesus Christ, Nelson Mandela, Mahatma Gandhi, Martin Luther King (Jnr.) are perfect examples of people who connected with their followers' problems.

How well you identify and understand people's problems and connect with them determines your win in the leadership game. And for identifying people's pain points, you can follow a straightforward principle called NICHE. I've taught the NICHE principle at corporations to their sales team, management, and entrepreneurs. NICHE helps you begin to understand what drives people's decisions and behaviors daily and develop stronger connections with them. NICHE stands for Need, Interest, Concern, Hope, and Expectation. Whether you are connecting with your boss, peers, team, clients, or vendors, NICHE is the foundation of all relationships at work. Once you understand the person's NICHE, it's easy to build a rapport and support each other.

It was the 25th wedding anniversary of Mr. and Mrs. Mathew. They decided to celebrate it between them, reviving old memories of togetherness of the life they started together in Southern California. In the evening, they decided to go for a stroll on the famous streets of Santa Barbara. While there, they stood and admired a vast, luxurious hotel built 11 years ago.

They decided to step in and have a look. While inside, the hotel manager greeted them with a smile and asked them how he could serve them. The couple smilingly said they were only looking at the hotel but did not have that kind of money to stay or even dine here. The manager got irritated with them and said rudely, 'why did you walk in when you can't afford it.' The couple apologized and walked toward the door to leave. Just then, the restaurant owner walked in through that same door and smiled at this couple. He stopped them to ask them their experience of staying and dining at his hotel. Mr. Mathew smiled at the owner, saying,

> you know Sir, twenty-five years ago, my wife and I started our lives here in Southern California. And our first dinner after marriage was at a small restaurant that was exactly where your big luxurious hotel stands today. It looks like that restaurant is no more. So we just came in to take a look. We cannot afford to dine or stay here.

The owner of the restaurant smiled and said, 'well, this is that tiny restaurant which by my hard work and grace of the Lord has today become one the of the finest luxury hotels in Southern California.' The owner asked them to follow him to the reception. 'He told the receptionist to give the couple the keys to the VIP suite for tonight and arrange a set of clothes for them and get them the best dinner and morning breakfast services.' He looked at the couple, took their hands in it, and said, 'My restaurants inaugurated ecstasy the same day 25 years ago, and you were our first guest. Let me help you celebrate your 25th wedding anniversary like never before. Please enjoy this complimentary stay.' Mr. and Mrs. Mathew had one of the best celebrations of their life.

I know of this incident because the hotel owner is a client and a good friend of mine. My friend connected with Mathew's problem using NICHE. He knew the couple's need and deep desire to celebrate their anniversary. He gauged their interest to have dinner together and their concern for money, with their hope to revive their old memories and the expectation to have a wonderful evening somewhere. Not only did my friend help them enjoy their anniversary, but also Mathews became a lifelong ambassador for this hotel. Anyone and everyone they spoke to now knows about this hotel. Sales increased massively for my friend.

Take a pause here and think of people around you – your boss, your team, your college, and your client. What problem do they have? What's their pain point? What issues are they facing that they want to resolve? Can you make their lives easier? Can you connect with their pain? When you click with people's pain, even if you might not have any solution, you have helped them reduce it by assisting them to share it. Someone rightly said, 'joy shared is multiplied, and pain shared is divided.'

Connect with people's problems, and you will connect with them for life. Many people in the corporate world feel that successful people became successful because of luck. That they worked hard and had the chance and resources by their side.

At a conference I was speaking at early this year in London, I met with Amanda, the vice president of a Fortune 500 company. During our lunch conversation, I learned that Amanda was a young vice president at 32 years of age. She had begun her career at the age of 24 as an intern and quickly rose to prominence in her field. Almost everyone on that lunch table said a common phrase—'You're so lucky, Amanda.' Chances are you've been on the giving and receiving end of this familiar phrase more than once. You're fortunate to receive an opportunity. For a job. For a travel experience. For your relationship. Why do we give luck all the credit? At least Amanda didn't. She made it very clear that the most significant reason behind her success is the connections and rapport she built with people at and outside of her workplace. I agreed and knew what she was saying was absolutely a fact.

The secret of success is to build solid and lasting connections that happen when you understand people's pain points. Questions are a tool we use to dig for something. Find something in common to converse further. Here are some questions to help you identify people's pain points.

1. What is your biggest current challenge?
2. What has prevented you from overcoming this challenge?
3. Would a product or service that is or is not currently available help you solve that challenge?
4. What takes up the most time in your day?
5. What roadblocks prevent you from achieving your top two business goals?

## THE DIVISION OF THOUGHTS

When I teach about the Law of Problems, I've always had people from the audience say, 'hey Payal; I have my list of problems and pain points that I need to manage. Why do I want to take on someone else's problems.' This thinking is the leading cause of us not being able to connect deeply with people. A share of 80% of our focus in life is self-directed. My goals. My problems. My feelings. What do people think about me? Am I doing good? How will the boss evaluate my performance in the following review? Do my friends like me or see me as irritating? Only 15% of the time is for others. In that too we think about others, what they did wrong, how they should behave. What they must or mustn't do. So what's remaining truly for others is only 5%. And in this 5%, we aren't understanding or listening to someone's problems. This is how our thoughts are divided. We are self-absorbed humans. This is why we have more significant conflicts at work, grudges, misunderstandings, stress, and burnout. No one thinks of the other.

Recently, I heard from a coaching client of mine that one of her team members missed a critical deadline on a substantial project. Unsurprisingly, she got furious at him and said harsh words. It wasn't until much later that we all learned that his wife and mother were battling Covid-19, and he was preoccupied, caring for them at home.

One CEO in my ICONX program, a coaching group for executives, talked about how, even though she knows her team is capable, she avoids delegating. And now she is exhausted from saving everyone from making mistakes and doing their work for them. Soon, she began to speak about her brother, who killed himself years earlier. Through tears, she told us of her regret at not being able to save him. It soon became evident that she was unable to save her brother; she was trying to keep everyone else, a habit draining her and preventing her company from succeeding.

H. Jackson Brown, Jr. said it well, 'remember that everyone you meet is afraid of something, loves something, and has lost something.' A while back, the *Wall Street Journal* published an article on the reasons that executives fail. At the top of the list was a person's inability to relate to others effectively.

We leaders are so pressured to make a decision and get results that we forget the human element of leadership. The division of our thoughts needs to be changed. Beautiful relations are built when we spend more of our time genuinely connecting with people, thinking about them, and trying to make a difference in their lives. While most people express their hopes and aspirations in terms like 'I hope I get' or 'I want to do,' successful leaders understand that it's we before I and us before me.

I'm reminded of the famous quote often attributed to Plato: be kind; everyone you meet is fighting a difficult battle. At work, connecting to another's humanity or another's pain creates bonds and builds trust, and fosters more authentic and open communication and greater creativity. Think about it. Wherever someone has connected with your problem or pain, how did it make you feel? Often we think that we are the only ones troubled by a multitude of problems. And think others are enjoying their lives. We forget that everyone has a fair share of their problems. And, perhaps, many are in a much worse state than you are.

How good is your ability to get people to open up and deeply connect with you? Knowing the art to understand the needs of others and being aware of their feelings and thoughts is a quality only a few leaders have but can be developed by one and all. Now let me tell you something here. It's not an easy job connecting with people's problems and their pain points. Because many people are terrified to open up about their deepest fears and insecurities. And many don't even realize they are in pain. The pain, the problem, has become such an integral part of their lives that they don't know it exists. Most people have 'shadow' parts they reveal only to very few other people. How many times have you as a leader asked someone, 'How are you?' and the response generally is 'am doing good.' In reality, you might even know that the person is feeling horrible. How many times have you hidden your true feelings?

It takes time and effort to connect with people based on their problems. When you take the time to establish rapport in this way, you open doors for other people to align themselves with you and your business' mission.

A six-figure entrepreneur I was once coaching gave me very sage advice. She said that people are moved either by desperation or inspiration. So I believe that if you can leverage either of these, it helps you to win people. Understanding human needs and emotions are the defining elements of building a strong rapport with people. Any good psychologist will tell you that one of the deepest needs of a human being is the need to belong.

Without empathy, you can't build a winning team. You will not inspire followers or elicit loyalty.

Let me share with you a simple tactic of three steps to connect with people's problems. I've taught this principle to executives and individual contributors, and it's helped them connect with people at the level of their problem and happiness. When socializing, networking at professional events, speaking with a boss, or selling to a client, apply the three-step connection formula and see the difference.

1. Listen and observe: Listen and watch for what's most important for others. What are their beliefs about life and work? What is something that motivates them toward pleasure and away from pain? Learn how they make decisions and what's most important in their world. I say, be a world-class listener. I remember here one of Nelson Mandela's articles I had read somewhere. It is said that Nelson Mandela would often accompany his father to the village meetings. He saw that all the people in the forum sat in a circle to see each other face to face. And another thing he observed is that his father would speak the last in that meeting. Nelson learned that listening and watching are most important to connect with people's problems or happiness.

2. Apply PAQ: Some years back I introduced the concept of PAQ, Power of Active Questions, to help leaders get to a win-win situation in most conversations.

    Great connectors spark catalytic questions that lead to break-through insights while taking a careful approach to not violating anyone's privacy. Questioning is a uniquely powerful tool for unlocking what's deep inside a person. Nothing has such power to cause a complete mental turnaround as that of a question. A powerful question is enough to cause a seismic mental shift—the type that precedes those glorious 'aha!' moments that come all too infrequently—and when your mindset changes, so too does your behavior. PAQ shows people that you are interested in what they have to say. Now, PAQ is not only to be applied to others.

3. Constantly check on others. See if they need any help. Check on their emotional well-being. Talk to them about their problems. What is it that's stopping them from giving their best?

Once you understand and master these three simple steps of accessing leverage to create change, you can use it in either your own life or to help someone you know the difference in an area that matters most.

We often want to skip over feeling pain entirely, choosing instead to work toward joy or a sense of closure. Most people try to build connections by using words. They talk about themselves and their work rather than getting to know the other person thoroughly well. The way of making lasting connections is through people's hearts and minds.

Research has shown that winning, being at the top of your game doesn't have to do with your role, title, job description, or the number of hours you work. It has everything to do with the quality and depth of your connections built. How you interact with your contacts is essential in determining your win.

## RAPID ACTION PLAN

Today onward each day make a conscious effort to connect with the problem of people who cross your way.

# 6

## Law of Transference

In the early years of establishing my coaching and training company, while coaching people experiencing leadership difficulties, my attitude was, 'Be fast and finish telling me your problem so I can give you my solution.' When I was leading any initiative, I constantly asked myself, 'How can I get people to buy into my vision so that they'll help me grow and succeed?' When I gave presentations, I was focused on myself and not my audience. I lived for the positive feedback. And my goal was always to be impressive. Much of what I did was all about me. Let me tell you, this attitude of mine did not take me too far in the early days of my career, and I know it doesn't take anyone ahead in their game either. I learned then that a leader's energy is transferred to the team and the organization. My energy of being is a state of rush and making it all about me transferred to my people, thereby distancing them from me.

Once while driving from my home in Raleigh toward Charlotte to give a keynote at a huge banking conference, I was stuck in traffic for a while. On the other side of the road, there was some construction going on. I watched a road crew at work. Now the team leader was having a bad day. A bus driver was hitting her horn because a traffic barricade was in her way. The team leader yelled, threw a fist into the air, and then kicked over the barricade. He indeed was one angry man.

Then he started yelling at his crew and mocking them, spitting out his venom. They looked down at the ground and kept on working. I sense they felt humiliated by the public spectacle. But the team leader continued his rant. I bet tonight he'll blame his crew for a low-performance day. And the anger and stress he has transferred to his people will be carried by the team to their colleagues and family members.

DOI: 10.4324/9781003260714-8

Not long ago, I coached an executive who was appointed as the CEO of a huge non-profit organization. I got to know that he was not a healthy nor a strong man. He was in a wheelchair, and he had a myriad of health problems. However, the organization he led was in dire trouble economically and eventually failed during the pandemic. And the simple fact is that the organization needed to draw strength from somewhere and someone during these challenging times. And that person was their CEO. The organization, its team, and its members needed to see stability and confidence from their leader, and they drew on that strength.

Eventually, and throughout his work, the organization began to grow stronger. He was transferring his strength to the organization he was leading. I call this the law of transference.

The law of transference says that as a leader, you will transfer to your people what is inside of you and whatever you are best at. It can be both positive and negative. You can be infected with someone's happiness or sadness. The entire culture of any organization is formed based on this law of transference.

A typical example of transference at the workplace is feeling worried that you cannot trust your current boss because an ex-boss broke your trust when you shared sensitive work issues. In this case, you are redirecting your feelings about that ex-boss onto your new one. Other examples include feeling annoyed at someone who reminds you of your client who nagged you on every mistake or being extra nice to someone from your team who reminds you of your father's positive qualities.

---

## IT'S A CYCLE

Once a highly successful businessman, running a health insurance company was getting ready to go to his office. When he reached into his car and opened the door, a stray dog sleeping under his car suddenly came out and bit on his leg! The businessman got very angry and quickly picked up a few rocks and threw at the dog but none hit the dog. The dog ran away.

Upon reaching his office, the businessman calls a meeting of his managers and during the meeting he puts the anger of the dog on them. The managers also get upset by the anger of their boss and they put their anger to the employees working under them. The chain of this reaction keeps going till the lower level of employees and finally, the anger reaches to the office peon.

Now, there was no one working under the peon! So, after the office time is over, he reaches his home, and wife opens the door. She asked him, 'Why are you so late today?' The peon, upset due to anger thrown at him by the staff, gives one slap to his wife! And says, 'I didn't go to the office to play football, I went to work so don't irritate me with your stupid questions!'

So, now the wife got upset that she got a scolding plus a slap for no reason. She puts her anger on his son who was watching TV and gives him a slap, 'This is all you do, you have no interest in studying! Turn off the TV now!'

The son gets upset now! He walks out of his house and sees a dog passing by looking at him. He picks up a rock and hits the dog in his anger and frustration. The dog, getting hit by a rock, runs away barking in pain.

This was the same dog that bit the businessman in the early morning.

This story is a great reminder that what goes around comes around. What we transfer from within us eventually comes back to us. Culture of a company is created by what you and I create daily at our work.

## WHAT ARE YOU CREATING?

People often complain to me that they are fed up with their work environment where there is negativity. And I immediately ask them, 'So what has been your contribution to this type of environment.' You see, it's easy to blame the management or the people around you for the hostile work environment. We forget that we contribute to this environment too. You see, my friend, no company sets its foundation on negativity. No CEO says that I am here to create a hostile work environment. Today despite the high security at our doors, negativity still enters our workforce. It enters through each of us. Whatever grudges, anxiety, fear, tension, joy, happiness, the calmness you bring with you to that meeting, to that zoom call, to that one on one, to that company is what creates the environment.

You are the master of your environment. You control your work environment by what you bring in and what gets transferred to others by you. As we know, self-awareness is essential for the success of any kind. You've got to understand yourself to utilize best who you are as a person. Self-awareness is more than looking inward, however. It's also looking outward and examining how you interact with the environment around you. Our thoughts and feelings shape our workplace. Our work environment, your teams are a reflection of what we have transferred. It's a reminder to each of us to invest in our well-being, development, and knowledge. Earl Nightingale said that whatever happens inside always happens outside.

While speaking at a medical conference in Portland, I heard from the physicians how many situations could elicit emotions in physicians in the daily routine of a hospital or a private practice. For instance, breaking bad news to a patient is often perceived as stressful by physicians. It is associated with both increased physiological arousal and difficulties in handling resulting emotions such as sorrow, guilt, or the feeling of failure. If they carry these feelings around with them, it surely gets transferred to the next patient, the nurse to the janitor, to just everyone around them. So, they must know how to manage what is inside of them.

## EMOTIONAL EQUILIBRIUM QUOTIENT

Most leaders fall prey to the 'me' trap. They feel it's about their day, emotions, feelings, results, and thoughts. And so, if the leader has a bad day, they vent it out on their teams, and if the leader has a good day, they show it to their teams. In both scenarios, it's all about what a leader carries within, which is transferred around.

Have you experienced how the team leader sets a tone for anger and behaves angrily with everyone? Or, if the leader shows anxiety, fear, or irritation, the team embraces the same behavior. Or when leaders blame everything and everyone for all mistakes, their teams never demonstrate ownership.

When the CEOs we interviewed for this chapter discussed some of the most pressured situations in their lives, one remarkable commonality was their use of emotional equilibrium to cope with transferring their negative and positive emotions to their teams, stakeholders, management, and clients. They realized that being highly cheerful or frustrated could lead to bad decisions and transfer the same feelings to their people.

Emotional equilibrium is your ability to stay clear-headed and see the situation as it is while exploring your emotional reactions to sources of tension.

Take this scenario: A soccer team is playing in a critical game and is down by one goal. Just before half-time, a player from the opposing team gets fouled, and the team is given a penalty kick—a great opportunity to tie up the score. A leading player on the team steps up to take the shot but loses it. Head in his hands, he walks off the field to meet his team for their half-time meeting.

The team is upset. The coach is disheartened. The coach aims to get the players over this hump, ready to return to the field feeling pumped and motivated. Whatever is inside of the coaches' heads and hearts will ultimately get transferred to the team players. The coach needs to maintain the emotional equilibrium by either getting too angry or faking to be calm. He needs to access the situation and get them ready to go out there and create history.

How many times in anger have you felt like throwing in your resignation letter? Have there been events in your life when you've been super excited and spilled the beans out too soon?

Now I know that leaders are real people, humans, and they too have their days and problems. And that leading through a fog of emotions is difficult. The truth is leaders have tough days, personal lives, frustration, moments of anger, fear, sadness, insecurity, and feel burn-out. Whether you are in a position of professional leadership, an entry-level employee, how, when, and where you vent these feelings in a way that protects your leadership, your reputation, your organization, and your relationships will set you apart from your average counterparts.

Here's the point I want to make right now. Whatever you carry inside of you is highly contagious. So know to stay on the line of emotional equilibrium, else you will go about transferring excessive happiness or excessive frustration to everyone around you. And that's how you see in your teams a reflection of yourself.

---

## POWER UP

It's easy to miss how the law of transference can impact our winning the leadership game. Leaders have a lot on their plate, from taking care of the budget, global teams, projects, growth, family, network connections, office meetings, and so much more. By the end of the day, you are drained out completely. The following day when you wake up, you get back into the day's cycle, and again by the time, it's time to go to bed, you are drained out. And the process continues. My question to you is, what have you done to power up yourself? If every day you are stressed out and drained out before going to bed, guess what? You wake up in the same state—with little energy. Many people feel if they have had a good night's sleep, their energy in the morning will be high. Not at all. It's not true. The fact is the state in which you sleep is the state in which you wake up. So say, for example, you slept in the form of 10% energy left in your reservoir. You will wake up with 20–30% energy in the morning, assuming you had a good night's sleep. That's it. Nothing more. If you want to wake up with 95% energy, if you're going to be of value to your team, your family, your organization, then you've got work to do here. Because it's not possible to add value to others' lives if you are constantly struggling internally or are empty from the inside. You can't make a difference in someone's life if you are drained out or if you allow people and circumstances to.

I know of a person who started his own IT consulting business. I saw how he had all the knowledge in the world about consulting. He would enroll himself in more learning to get more knowledge. Well, that's great. But he never shared his knowledge with people until he would get paid for it. And guess what, people did not pay him because they did not know how good he was at his work. They did not know what value he could add to their lives. So he was full of knowledge with no space for new information to flow into him. Add to it he was constantly struggling in his own life and was always drained out. How do you think he could offer to consult anyone? Who would benefit from his work?

As leaders, we have a lot to give and a lot to learn. It's a cycle in our lives. If we are full of problems and anxiety, we cannot add value to anyone, even though we might be very intellectual.

Many human resource professionals have asked me this question, 'Payal, do you ever get impacted by your clients' problems?' And my answer is no for most of the time.

It doesn't mean that leaders don't experience 'dry seasons.' In my work of traveling and helping people with their leadership problems, I feel the exhaustion and depletion that occurs after giving and serving.

*There is a famous story I've heard about a wise Zen master. People trav-eled from far away to seek his help. In return, he would teach them and show them the way to enlightenment. On this particular day, a scholar came to*

*visit the master for advice. 'I have come to ask you to teach me about Zen,'*
*the scholar said.*

*Soon, it became apparent that the scholar was full of his own opinions and*
*knowledge. He interrupted the master repeatedly with his own stories and*
*failed to listen to what the master had to say. The master calmly suggested*
*that they should have tea.*

*So the master poured his guest a cup. The cup was filled, yet he kept running*
*until the cup overflowed onto the table, onto the floor, and finally onto the*
*scholar's robes. The scholar cried, 'Stop! The cup is full already. Can't you see?'*

*'Exactly,' the Zen master replied with a smile. 'You are like this cup—so*
*full of information that nothing more will fit in. Come back to me with an*
*empty cup.'*

I think of this story often because it reminds me that we fill up our cups
with our past experiences and knowledge as we get older. Whatever knowledge and expertise you have, share it for the good of others. Don't let it fill
the space in your brain. Create space in your brain to fill it with new information. And every night before going to bed, I empty my cup again—my
cup of problems, worries, and anxiety. I give it to the Lord to take care
of them.

It would help if you had an essential daily routine for having your leadership cup filled and emptied. It's easy to go through our work life holding
on to the things that weigh us down like jealousy, negativity, anxiety, work
pressure, deadlines, pandemic, and so much more. That's taking up space
for the good things that belong to you, and it's getting transferred to others
around you. If you fill your cup with worry, there is no space for creativity.
There's no space for both. Most people don't win the game because they
don't practice the art of filling and emptying their cups. Most of us are
taught to keep serving our cups.

From the early years of our education life until we are alive, we are only
filling our cups. We are filled with new information and keep the old data
and beliefs. How many of us even use that outdated information and beliefs
stored in our minds? We are never taught to follow the cycle of filling and
emptying our cups. Seventy-five percent of our cup is filled with negativity,
grudges, and old information, leaving only 25% for new creativity and
information. The scripture says, 'give no place to the enemy,' which means
anything that weighs you down or contaminates your thinking.

I remind myself daily that we've all come empty-handed in this world, and
we all will leave empty-handed from this world. None of us are guaranteed

a tomorrow. My father says we all have an expiry date, but we don't know that date. So why not practice to sleep empty each night of our worries, tensions, problems, our pride, and our belongings and if we are blessed to wake up in the morning, I assure you that you will wake up powered up to seize the day. And it is this power and vigor that you will transfer to people.

Here's what you want to do. In the daytime, empty your cup of knowledge and expertise by sharing it with those who would benefit from it. And fill your cup with new skills, knowledge, and information that will help you win the game. Every night before you sleep, empty your cup filled with worry, tension, pride and instead fill it with gratitude. You see, gratitude changes our perspective and outlook on life. It's impossible to be thankful and negative at the same time. This way, when you wake up in the morning, you feel light from inside.

One of the most powerful practices I have derived which have helped CEOs and executives is the practice of self-optimization. The diagram below is very self-explanatory. It will show you what you must do each morning as you wake up and every night before bed. It will give you the duration of each practice.

Self-Optimization

**FIGURE 6.1**
Self-Optimization Wheel

## SELF-OPTIMIZATION

Practice this routine for a week and see the difference. You will wake up each morning powered up 100% ready to learn and prepared to add value to people's lives. You will be an MVP—The most valuable person at your workplace. You are paid for the value you bring in both in the marketplace and in the lives of people. Be a person who is willing to play full out.

## RAPID ACTION PLAN

Take some time daily to practice self-optimization using the optimization wheel.

# 7

## Law of Mirror

What do people want out of work? More than money, more than benefits, much more than job security, a recent survey says, they want to be treated with respect. Be it anyone in any position, being treated with respect has been rated as one of the essential needs of people.

A few years ago, while coaching the daycare owner, a statement she often repeated to her staff was, 'I want you to treat me with respect.' Once over lunch, I asked her why she often repeated this statement, and she said, 'Payal, I am the owner of this daycare, and I want to be respected,' I smiled and asked her, 'so you want people to respect you because you are the owner. What if you were not the owner? Would you want them to respect you any differently?'

I have met many people who want respect because of their position, power, or money. My mother would often say; respect is to be commended, not demanded. I agree. And you command respect with your actions. The way people treat you is not dependent on them; it's dependent on you.

One of the complaints I often hear from people is that they feel their boss doesn't value them. I ask them what makes them say that. They say they work hard, take up more work, and do everything it takes to show their ability and skills. In return, their boss only gives them more jobs. They feel unappreciated and undervalued. After hearing them, my response is a simple two-line sentence—your attitude toward yourself reflects others. People treat you the way you unconsciously treat yourself. That's the law of the mirror. The Law of the Mirror proposes that the origin of whatever happens to us is a reflection of what we give out. What you see in yourself is what others see in you. This law says that whatever you are willing to put up with and however you allow yourself to be treated is precisely what you will have. You get what you give out.

DOI: 10.4324/9781003260714-9

Because you are showing your boss that you are OK with taking up extra work every time, so your boss gives you more work because they think you can handle it. The question you must ask yourself then is why am I taking up so much work? Maybe you are afraid of losing your job; perhaps you want to please your boss; maybe you think it may lead to a promotion, or perhaps you are simply a workaholic.

Whatever be the reason, remember you are treated as you treat yourself. It's the law of the mirror.

Your people value you based on how you love yourself. Now I am not saying you shouldn't take up extra work or work hard. But suppose you constantly take up work during your scheduled time off or continuously oblige to take on complex tasks from other workers but aren't compensated for it. In that case, you subtly show your value and signal how you should be treated. Remember, people take signs and signals from you on how they should treat you. So, pay very close attention to the signals you are giving out.

Let's say, for example, that you have a coworker who constantly takes credit for your ideas or goes out of his way to throw you under the bus. Or maybe someone is always rude to you or is taking you for granted. These people behave that way because they're getting some sign from you that this is how you should be treated and that you are OK with it. Otherwise, they'd stop.

So here's a rule of thumb. To win the leadership game, begin to treat yourself better, and others will follow suit. Begin today to treat yourself the way you want to be treated. You want your time to be respected by others, then start by respecting your time first. Want to be appreciated by others? Then enjoy yourself instead. Talk about your accomplishments without being bashful. Want your work to be valued? Then choose to believe in yourself and focus not on your weaknesses but your strengths. Live your life by using your skills and strengths unique to you instead of fretting about the things you're not good at. You are valuable and worthy just as you are born to be. Don't let your doubts and comparisons get in your way.

Here's one mantra I often repeat to myself; 'people consciously treat you the way you unconsciously treat yourself.' So if you want to be a world-class leader, if you wish your boss, your team, your clients to respect you and value your work—here's the deal—treat yourself in ways that set standards for others. Pay close attention to yourself. Take a pause here and reflect on these questions:

What is your energy telling people about you?
What is your attitude saying about you and how you view life?
What is your self-care or lack thereof telling people about how you treat yourself?

## A LEADER'S MIRROR

In today's fast-paced, complex world, leaders need mirrors. The mirrors they need, however, go far beyond reflecting their physical appearance. Leaders need mirrors that reflect their behavior and the impact their behavior has on others. We need mirrors that will help us grow internally so we can manifest externally.

Have you ever looked into the leadership mirror and asked yourself why you are where you are in life? Have you reached some or any of the dreams that you imagined as a child? I'm not talking about the American dream of a big house with a branded car in the driveway, and a high-paying job, unless, of course, that is your dream, which is fine. What I am talking about is where you are in terms of your purpose in your life. Are things stacking up the way you expected them to?

I believe that if I had understood the Law of the Mirror at a younger age, I would be further along than I am now. When I was young, I never really thought I suffered from low self-esteem. As I got older, I indeed realized that I needed to work on things. Most people do not reach their full potential due to low self-esteem.

A few years back, I was coaching an entrepreneur who runs online Math classes for college students. She was excellent at her work and wanted me to help her expand her business. During the coaching, I learned she was very frustrated with how her husband and kids treated her. She felt they did not respect her work and work timings. She felt they treated her poorly and took her and her work for granted. But today, she is a confident woman who is successful in her business and, above all, is treated with respect and dignity by her family, including being highly valued. What brought about this change in her behavior? Apart from advising her on how to lead her business, I taught her to look into the leader's mirror that changed her life—both professionally and personally. It's the same mirror I applied in my life to raising my self-esteem. It's the very same mirror I taught a client of mine to look into who is a successful fashion designer for Hollywood actors and who, in her early career life, went through a phase of being treated like trash in the media industry. It's a leader's mirror of discovery.

A leader's discovery mirror is an internal mirror to look at yourself and work on yourself. It's a space not for a monologue but a dialogue. It's a rich, delicious, courageous conversation you have with yourself. A leader's discovery mirror is two fields: one where you discover your strengths and weaknesses and the other where you appreciate yourself.

You can discover your strengths and weaknesses by looking into the mirror of discovery and asking yourself three powerful questions:

- What kind of a leader am I?
- What kind of a leader do I want to be?
- What do I want to be known for?

You can then look into the discovery mirror and appreciate yourself by coming up with an ending for the following sentences. Start each sentence with your name.

'_____, I am proud of you for ....'

'_____, I forgive you for ....'

'_____, I love you for ....'

Be very honest with yourself when completing these sentences because your answers to both of the above sets will reflect the feelings you have about yourself. It makes you immediately aware of where you are resisting and where you are open and flowing. It clearly shows you what thoughts you will need to change if you want to have a joyous, fulfilling life.

Your outer world is a direct reflection of your inner world. If you want to change the world you see, start working on your inner world. Your reality is merely a mirror reflecting your inner world.

---

## YOU GET WHAT YOU TOLERATE

You see, my friend, people know your boundaries; they know your hot buttons. They learn to what level you will tolerate their behavior. So fundamentally, what you allow will continue. You have to love and respect yourself and what you do, and you've got to know yourself enough so that you can discontinue, reject, refuse anything that you should no longer allow in your life—including people. When you sit in solitude and look into the discovery mirror for your strengths, weaknesses, and what you appreciate yourself for, you will discover your true self. You will know the reason for your low self-esteem. You will know when to set your boundaries.

Most people blame their spouse, boss, client, friends, parents, team, and circumstances for being treated. In life, you will meet people. People who judge you, who love and care for you, and those who hate you. You must set your boundaries as to what you allow and what you don't.

My husband and I were at a favorite restaurant in town that often seems to have a problem understaffed due to constant staff absenteeism. We've heard, on several occasions, that they have a problem with servers simply calling in at the last minute. As the manager ran around like a chicken searching for its head, I desperately wanted to tell the manager to look into the leader's discovery mirror and ask four questions. Because if he keeps allowing his workers to treat him like this, the restaurant, and their coworkers with such blatant disrespect, they will. He needs to set his boundaries, which will happen only when he lifts the mirror of discovery.

If you continue to allow what you have always allowed, you will continue to get what you have always gotten. If you want different results in your life or work, all you have to do is pick up the leader's discovery mirror and change what you want. So here's some work for you. Stop reading ahead and fill in the table below with the four questions.

As you finish filling in this table, ask yourself; have I set my boundaries? Developing and sustaining boundaries is a skill necessary for winning. Unfortunately, it's a skill that many of us don't learn. A boundary is a

**TABLE 7.1**

A Leader's Discovery Mirror

| What are you tolerating? | What is the reason/s for tolerating? | What is the cost of tolerating? | What is your new decision and action? |
| --- | --- | --- | --- |
| | | | |

personal property line, or limit, that defines where you end, and someone else begins. Think of your home or your apartment. There is a property line, and you are in control of what goes on there, who is allowed to visit, and on and on. In short, you have control. No trespassing.

The harsh reality is if you don't set boundaries clearly, you will end up with many things on your 'property'—your life—that you did not invite and certainly do not want.

## CREATE BOUNDARIES, NOT WALLS

Because everyone who wants to come into our lives may not be suitable for us, we can decide whether to allow them to get close to us or not. This kind of boundary setting can be physical, but it can also be emotional and mental. We get to decide whether or not we will give certain people access to our hearts and minds. We can choose how much we will allow our hearts to love or trust them—if at all. We can also decide how much we will think about them. One of the keys to being a healthy individual is to have appropriate boundaries in relationships.

There is a difference between boundaries and walls, and sometimes when a person is wounded in their soul, they'll put up walls instead of setting boundaries. Let me explain the difference. A person who puts up walls says to themselves: 'I've been hurt before, and nobody is ever going to hurt me again! I am not going to allow anyone to get close to me ever again. That way, they can't hurt me.' Great leaders don't build walls.

A person who sets healthy boundaries says: 'I have experienced a lot of hurt in my life, and I need to protect myself and be involved with people who are safe for me. I am going to be wise and cautious as I build relationships.'

Do you see the difference between building walls and setting boundaries? Building walls leaves no room for healthy relationships because it closes off the possibility of close relationships completely. A person who sets boundaries is open to deep relationships, but only if they are respectful and beneficial.

Think of boundaries like lines on the highways, which provide margins for our safety while we're driving. If we go over one side, we'll go into the ditch. If we cross over the line in the middle, we could get killed. And we like those lines because they help to keep us safe. Sometimes we don't even realize how lines help to keep us safe.

Similarly, when we begin to have boundaries, borders, and margins in our personal lives, we experience more peace, energy, better relationships, and higher productivity.

To identify your physical, emotional, mental, and spiritual limits, lack of boundaries allowed me to give my energy, time, power, and money to others, leaving virtually nothing for myself. Living without boundaries, overworking myself to the point of burnout, trying to please everyone, battling with money, creating healthy boundaries means that you take responsibility for yourself, your time, your feelings, and your energy instead of allowing yourself to be buffeted around by everyone else's.

Boundaries allow you to take control rather than allow others to control you, and, conversely, you will give more to others because you come from a place of abundance rather than lack.

To create boundaries for yourself, you have to tune in to your personal needs and true feelings.

We govern what our minimum standards are by what we tolerate. Let me give you an example from my own life. In the early years of my career, I had this lady colleague in my office who would make a mistake, get yelled at by our boss, cry, and rinse and repeat. She asked me why the boss never yelled at me, and I said,

> When I make a mistake, I own it. I don't crumble or get flustered. I immediately figure out how to rectify it and move on. Plus, he knows that I will not allow anybody to yell at me. Do you know your boundaries? Only when you are aware of your boundaries can you say no confidently to things that you don't want to tolerate.

The law of the mirror says you are treated and allow other people to treat you. When you set boundaries or cut off contact with those who do not meet those expectations, you are setting the standard for relationships in your life. If you are willing to tolerate mistreatment, you will be mistreated. If you are ready to tolerate unhappiness, you will remain unhappy. If you are willing to tolerate dissatisfaction, you will stay dissatisfied. If you are OK tolerating a rude boss, you will be treated like dirt.

Your life becomes the sum of what you tolerate. You can change the way people treat you by changing the way you treat yourself.

## RAPID ACTION PLAN

Write down all the things you've been tolerating at your work and in life. Once you have your list ready, now pick one item from this list and begin to take action that will help you equip yourself with confidence to move ahead.

# 8

## Law of Visibility

The year I got promoted to a leadership role, I remember I was super excited. Not just for myself but also for me. You see, I've always been a person who wants people to achieve success in what they do. So I started encouraging my team to grow, climb upward and see what I see from the top. The more I did that, the more I found myself distancing myself from them. I could not understand why they weren't motivated to climb upward when I told them exactly what to do. Who wouldn't love the fact that you have someone telling you the exact steps you need to take to become successful. For months I could not understand what was wrong. Then one evening, while sitting at a café, sipping my favorite Chocolate Java Chip Frappuccino, still thinking about why my team wasn't showing any interest in growing, I saw something that fascinated me. While the staff was busy taking orders, making coffee, billing, and delivering, the manager of the café was with her team at the back of the counter, showing them precisely what to do, how to do and enjoying with them while taking them ahead in their game. I loved the smiles on their faces.

I took my eyes and attention off them and focused on my problem—why aren't my people like this team at Starbuck. Why aren't they enjoying moving ahead in their game? Almost eight months had passed in this role of mine, and by now, I was getting slightly frustrated with my situation.

The following month my company organized a leadership training session for which I and a few others from the company were sent to London for three days. One evening, we decided to go to this well-known Indian restaurant in Southall. Now, if you've been to London, you know that South Hall is the hub for the South-Asian community. While at the restaurant, we fell in love with the traditional décor and authentic food. While the server served us ice-cold water, the owner of the restaurant came

DOI: 10.4324/9781003260714-10

and introduced himself. He spoke with us as if he had known us for years. We learned about his family, his other chain of restaurants in London, the best dish we should order, and his accomplishments. He even gave us a tour of his kitchen and took some pictures with us. I saw his servers and cooks were so fulfilled with their work. They seemed like a replica of the owner because they too engaged in a conversation with us and had this contagious smile all over their face even at 10.30 pm. Seeing him and his team made me think of my problem with my team. Why aren't they doing what I tell them? We took his leave and waited for a cab outside the restaurant. When he knew that we weren't getting any cabs to get to the main street, he spoke to his team, took out his car, and drove us to the main road, which was no more than 10 minutes from his restaurant. We thanked him profoundly. Later I got to know that he is very well known for his attitude.

On my flight back to the United States, sitting in silence near the window seat, I was still thinking about my team's problem. A year passed by. My problem continued, and I felt a leadership block. You know that block, right, where you have the knowledge and expertise but feel stuck and stagnated. Yes, that's what I was experiencing. It is said that when you want something, and it's one of the most dominant thoughts in your mind, the universe helps you connect with a solution or the pathway. And that's what happened to me. It was a usual Wednesday. I came home from work. While still thinking of my problem, I made myself hot coffee when my subconscious mind took me down the memory lane to the Starbuck manager and the London restaurant owner's experiences. And at that exact moment, I don't know from where I stopped turning the newspaper pages, and my eyes fell on an article written on Mother Teresa, and something that struck me in that article were these words—*she lived among us. She is one of us, someone who we saw alive living among us as an ordinary being.* Yes, I said to myself thoughtfully. Yes, of course. That's what the Starbucks manager and the restaurant owner of London did. They lived among their people—their clients, their team. They did not just tell them what to do or show them how to do it. They lived daily among them. They laughed with them; they shared their concerns; they connected with their heart to heart, mind to mind. In short, they were visible at their people's level—whatever be their level. They were practicing the law of visibility. I was only standing at the mountain top, shouting words of encouragement, and telling them to come up. No one heard me. No one was interested. I was like what the famous poet Saint Kabir quotes, 'What is the benefit of growing as big as a palm tree, which cannot give shade to anyone properly, nor are its fruits accessible.'

Being visible is a daily process and an intentional one.

That day onward, I practiced the law of visibility, and I consciously began going down the mountaintop to where my people were. I became visible to my team, not just physically but mentally. I made it a point to talk face to face or through the phone or video chat with every direct report. I also strategically reached out to indirect reports to continue to build those relationships. I lived with my team. And I walked up with them. And believe me when I say, when you practice the law of visibility. My problem shrank to the size of a mole. I empowered my team to identify what needs to be done and do it. However, there were boundaries in regards to people, operational interruptions, and costs. When setting boundaries, I was careful not to shut myself off from the team. I met with each direct report weekly and conducted one-on-one coaching sessions to set, adjust and create goals and objectives, conduct ongoing performance reviews, and develop a mentoring relationship. I make sure to collaborate with those outside of my direct reports and team. I made it a priority to meet with every department head once a month to listen to their concerns and suggestions and share information. And since then, I have practiced the law of visibility.

The law of visibility means leading by being visible. It is not about just being seen by your people. It's not about the open door policy where people can come to talk to you. It's not about simply wandering the halls or dropping an email saying 'hi' to everyone, showing your face and making sure people 'see' you, or maybe engaging in 'trivial' type conversations that neither person will recall later. It's far from simply sticking your neck out mindlessly at any cost to be seen. And it's not about just showing up in front of your management or being in their circle.

And sure enough, it's not even being seen at the right place at the right time. The law of visibility transcends all of these business mantras the corporate world has fed us. You are not reading this book to play average. You are here to be a winner every time. So you must go beyond what the general business mantras say about leadership and visibility.

Being visible means being where your people are and making a difference in the lives of those your cross paths with.

Today, being good at your job isn't the only requisite for getting ahead in your game. If key people aren't aware of you, you'll likely miss out on opportunities. And critical people are not only those in positions above you. The key people are your teams, colleagues, the security guard, the reception, the janitor. Winning the leadership game means you are visible at all levels, making an actual difference.

Let me share with you an incident with a friend of mine who is the CEO at an ice factory plant in Chicago. One evening while on his regular rounds to check if everything in the ice units was functioning well, he got inside a plant to check for any unwarranted leakage. As he entered the team, the door shut itself and got locked from the outside. He tried reaching for help, but all the employees had left for the day as it was 5.30 pm. My friend shared his experience of being locked in a room where the temperature inside was—10°C. Soon he began feeling the lack of oxygen, difficulty in breathing, and feeling dizzy. He remembers falling to the ground and feeling uneasy when the security guard opened the door and helped him out, giving him medical attention. My friend thanked the security guard immensely for saving his life and asked him how he knew he was stuck inside this plant. The guard said,

> Sir, every morning when you enter the gate, you smile at me and wish me good morning, and every evening as you leave, you smile and wish me good night. Sir, you've done this regularly since I was appointed here, now three and half years. Today, I heard your good morning but not your good evening. I was sure something was wrong, and I set out to check.

Hearing my friends' incident, I realized that visibility is not something you need to focus on only at the top. It's at all levels. My friend was visible enough to the security guard. He had made a difference in the life of the gatekeeper by greeting him daily.

In yet another incident, a client, Simon, mentioned his story to me during his executive coaching session. A promotion opportunity recently came up in Simon's department. The job matched his skills perfectly, and he truly knew his work well, so he was shocked when he didn't get an interview, especially when he learned that the successful candidate was less experienced than him.

When Simon asked his boss why he hadn't been considered for the role, she said she included the company's reception with her in the selection. The receptionist didn't know anything about Simon. Conversely, the successful applicant was well known to the reception—in terms of his family, abilities, and skills and had built strong connections with influential people. They had represented the department at company-wide gatherings. As a result, they knew what he could do.

---

## SLOW DOWN TO BE VISIBLE

Most executives tell me that they feel like they are running a 100-m dash all day long every day and need some clones to keep up [with] the pace. It's undeniably true that our ability to get stuff done and deliver results is what has made us successful in our careers. It has brought us to where we are today. However, if you continue to keep moving with speed, you will miss many valuable things on the way. You might miss the needs of the people, the joy and celebration of your team, the togetherness of your people. You might just miss your growth plan.

*The way we operate today reminds me of this story I read about a young and successful executive traveling down a neighborhood street, going a bit too fast in his new Jaguar. He was watching for kids darting out from between parked cars and slowed down when he thought he saw something. As his car passed, no children appeared. Instead, a brick smashed into the Jag's side door! He slammed on the brakes and drove the Jag back to the spot where the brick had been thrown. The angry driver then jumped out of the car, grabbed the nearest kid, and pushed him up against a parked car, shouting, 'What was that all about, and who are you?*

*Just what the heck are you doing?*

*That's a new car, and that brick you threw will cost a lot of money.*

*Why did you do it?'*

*The young boy was apologetic. 'Please, mister ... please, I'm sorry... I didn't know what else to do,' he pleaded.*

*'I threw the brick because no one else would stop....'*

*With tears dripping down his face and off his chin, the youth pointed to a spot just around a parked car.*

*'It's my brother,' he said.*

*'He rolled off the curb and fell out of his wheelchair, and I can't lift him.'*

*Now sobbing, the boy asked the stunned executive, 'Would you please help me get him back into his wheelchair? He's hurt, and he's too heavy for me.'*

*Moved beyond words, the driver tried to swallow the rapidly swelling lump in his throat. He hurriedly lifted the disabled boy back into the wheelchair, then took out his fancy handkerchief and dabbed at the fresh scrapes and cuts. A quick look told him everything was going to be okay.*

*'Thank you, and may God bless you,' the grateful child told the stranger.*

*Too shook up for words, the man simply watched the little boy push his wheelchair-bound brother down the sidewalk toward their home. It was a long, slow walk back to the Jaguar. The damage was very noticeable, but the driver never bothered to repair the dented side door. He kept the dent there to remind him of this message: Don't go through life so fast that someone has to throw a brick at you to get your attention!*

I want you to take a deep breath and pause before you read further. I urge you to ask yourself today, right now, at this moment, what are the things you've missed while you were in speed to get to where you want to be in your career? To be visible, you've got to be seen at the right place and the right time, not only for your growth and success but truly also the right place and time to make a difference.

At a conference in Singapore where I had to do a keynote, I had the opportunity to be a part of their delegate private dinner meeting. There I met one of Asia's top CEOs. During our candid conversation, I asked him the secret of his outrageous success at a young age. He smiled and answered in one sentence, 'I make time to reflect.' Every morning, he spends at least 45 minutes with his eyes closed, deep in reflection. I was just thinking. Sometimes he's analyzing business challenges. Other times he's thinking about new markets. At other times, he's being introspective on the meaning of his life and what he wants it to stand for. Often, he's simply dreaming up new ways to grow. You cannot grow and move forward if you do not know how to take a step back and reflect. It's all about slowing down to be visible. How much of your time do you spend slowing down and reflecting on the many different aspects of your life? This way, you will make yourself visible to your success.

## LEAD BY VISIBILITY

Lead by visibility (LBV) means that you are visible top-down, positively impacting the lives of people. It means you enjoy being around people. You are visible where they are. Rather than expecting them to move and expecting them to come to you for their needs, problems, or a heart-to-heart talk, you've got to go where they are LBV or leading by visibility is about consciously finding the opportunity to connect with people authentically. Most leaders are associated with people at the superficial level. LBV is all about honest conversations that leaders engage in with their people daily to find out what is happening for them. LBV, when done correctly, enables each individual to be at their best and deliver and meet or exceed targets.

This law is based on the hierarchical needs of the people. When practicing the law of visibility, connecting with people is of utmost importance. You must have what I call a people's plan. To better connect with people, you must be aware of their career hierarchy and start connecting with them where they are. Don't stand on the mountain top, thinking you are visible enough and giving them directions on getting to the top. Honestly, you don't even know if they want to get to the top. Knowing where they are on the career needs and being visible to them at that level is crucial to winning the leadership game.

1. Transformational needs: Working toward a higher purpose, has a sense of fulfillment
2. Self-development need: Aims to reach full potential, looks for mentorship and upskilling

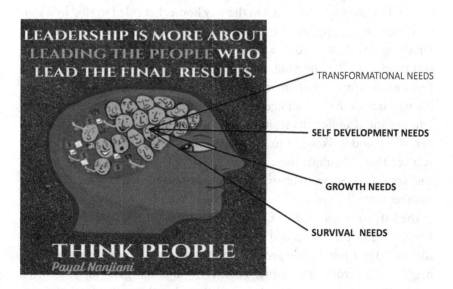

**FIGURE 8.1**
The Need Levels

3. Growth needs: Looks for title, position, achievement, higher income
4. Survival needs: Concerned with job security, pay, and trainings

Which level are you at? At what level is your team operating? What your influence will be on people depends on where you and they are on this pyramid. Those who are at the Survival level have different needs than someone who is at the self-development level. For you to win the game, you must understand who operates at what level.

A great leader is visible daily at all levels. It's a daily process, and it's an intentional process. The best strategy now is to figure out how to raise your visibility at work—in positive ways. You want to get noticed at work—both online and offline.

## THE DIFFERENCE IS IN MAKING A DIFFERENCE

One of the common myths people have about visibility is that one must do something big, something great, for someone to be visible. Rhea showed me that everyday acts of kindness go a long way in being visible.

I was returning to my hotel room one evening after an executive coaching session in downtown Atlanta. On the way home, I decided to stop by a grocery shop to pick up some fruits for my flight back home to Raleigh the following day. I stopped at a local grocery shop, picked up a few fruits, and headed to the checkout counter. There were six counters open, and I was wondering why counter number three had an enormous queue. On my way out to the car, an aged lady from that shop accidentally bumped into me and dropped the fruits she had picked up from the shop. I helped her with it and walked her to her car. On the way to her car, I told her, 'did you see that ridiculous huge line on check out number three. Five other checkout counters were open; I wonder why people were stuck at counter number three?'

The lady smiled and said, 'Oh, don't you know, it's because of the bagger, Rhea.' She has a nerve-related disease. To earn a living and be independent, she took up a job at this grocery shop. Initially, she was like any other bagger going from one cashier counter to another, greeting customers, putting their groceries in the bag, and thanking them. But from the past eight months, something changed. When I went home and emptied my grocery bag, I found an inspirational quote with Rhea's name on it. And this repeated every time I went to the store and was checked out by Rhea. So I make it a point to go to that counter where Rhea is a bagger, and I am sure that's the reason why others are doing it too. We all just love to get that new inspirational quote from her in our grocery bags. It truly makes my day. I've also heard that people get the answers to the problems in her quotes, 'Oh, she's making such a difference in the lives of people.'

By now, we had reached the lady's car; she thanked me for my help, blessed me, and drove away. While walking toward my car I thought about Rhea. I went back into the shop, picked up something I didn't really need, and stood in that long line to see what all this was about. And indeed, that day, the quote I got from her changed my thinking too. I still have the chit with me. It reads, 'the more you help others, the more abundance flows your way.' I never got an opportunity to pass that way again. But I still remember the value she added to my life that evening.

Rhea was visible to everyone. From her store manager to the customers at the grocery shop.

I've seen people wait to do something big to make a difference. And in that waiting, I've seen they never get the opportunity. You must look for ordinary ways to be extraordinary (that's a powerful formula for winning). The value you add to people's lives doesn't have to be grand or elaborate deeds (until, of course, you want to). Do the little things with unimaginable passion and off-the-scales intention.

In one of her interviews, Indra Nooyi, the CEO of PepsiCo, said she writes more than 400 letters of gratitude each year to the parents of her senior executives, and they have had quantifiable results.

Rohit, a software engineer, would often leave a chocolate bar at his desk with a Thank You note for the cleaning lady. She would always leave with a smile after cleaning his desk.

In my own life, I've met many people who have provided value in my life without any position, title, money, or status quo. And one of them was a mailman. My work involves a lot of travel. I am out of my home and city most of the days, and at times out of the country. The mailman who delivers mail at our home in North Carolina, rather than just leaving it in the mailbox, sorts out the mail for me in order of utility bills, magazines, coupons, etc. and ties each of the categorized emails with different colored satin ribbons with a personalized message on each. When I return home from my business travels, I always have a smile on my face seeing everything arranged and kept in a bin at my doorstep. Indeed, it just makes my life so much easier when I don't have to sort out the emails on my return.

When you provide value to others, your success grows organically. People seek more from you, talk about you to others, and share your amazing resources with their connections. And then you've grown exponentially. You genuinely are winning the leadership game every day. As is said in the scriptures, *Let each of you look not only to his interests but also to the interests of others.*

Every day I remind my team that we are in the business of making a difference. A great leader adds value to people. The effects are immeasurable. It creates high-performing employees. It grows a company from the inside out. It gives everyone a more fulfilling life. The most excellent way to effectively lead people is by finding ways to make a difference in their lives.

Every morning when you wake up, you have two options—either make people's lives better or make them worse. Which one do you choose daily? Being visible at your workplace happens in small daily ways before you get ample visibility. It's about making a difference every day.

Can you envision the unique work culture this kind of thinking would generate? Everybody would be helping each other to succeed. It would be a win for all. It is more sustainable when everyone wins. The outcome will be a happier, healthier, and high-performing culture.

Being visible is something that people struggle with. But the reality is that visibility is the only thing that will make you stand out from the masses when you contribute for a larger cause than your personal agenda. The simple but hard truth is that your business or your work is not unique. Someone is already doing it, and maybe even better than you if you compare purely with numbers.

But there is one crucial difference—there is only one of you. Your business, your work is not unique, but you certainly are. The only way to cut through the clutter and noise of your competition is to make yourself visible and relevant. Ten or twenty years from now, people need to look at you and think, wow, they have come a long way and are still rocking and relevant.

The more you put yourself out there, raw and honest, the better your chances of winning the leadership game.

## RAPID ACTION PLAN

What small acts are you going to do each day that will make a difference in someone's life?

# 9

## Law of Energy

Do you want to perform at a higher level? Do you want to get more done? In less time? Yes, of course, Payal, you might be saying. So what do you do about this? You work harder and work more. Give it your all. Don't stop when you are tired; stop when you are done. Rest in your graveyard only. Push yourself every day. Haven't we all been told these statements in an attempt to keep us motivated to be high achievers? True that these statements make some excellent quotes, but they don't make a successful leader.

Do you know how many hours a week a CEO typically works? According to a 12-year *Harvard Business Journal* study of 27 CEOs published last year, they work 62.5 hours a week and conduct business on 79% of weekend days, on average. To keep fit mentally for such intensive schedules, many CEOs and entrepreneurs herald the importance of taking time off to recharge, reenergize, and reconnect so they can come back energized and full of ideas. True, a vacation, dinner outing, spa treatment, and going off to a retreat rejuvenated us. However, I've observed these are short lives.

Every new era of business sees unique challenges and opportunities. A leader who consistently wins the leadership game can make the best out of the challenges and opportunities and adapt quickly to the changing business environment.

In all of my leadership talks and executive coaching, among all the inner leadership competencies I speak about, the law of energy is the most fundamental of all laws. If you do not apply the law of energy in your life, you cannot accomplish the other laws mentioned in this book. The law of energy's basic principle is that achieving anything worthwhile in your career requires a high level of physical, mental, and spiritual power.

DOI: 10.4324/9781003260714-11

The law of energy is based on a simple equation

IPE = PEE - UWE

Initial potential energy (IPE) = productively engaging energy (PEE) - unproductive wasted energy (UWE)

When we wake up in the morning, each has our IPE. The percentage of IPE varies in each person. Your IPE is dependent on the amount of productively expended energy and wasted energy from the previous day. It's why you will find that even after sleeping for long hours, some people are just not energetic. The number of hours a person sleeps does not generate more energy. The energy level is a result of the PEE and UWE.

Here's a big idea. The more you use your brain, the more energy you consume. The brain draws fuel, oxygen, and glucose, from blood delivered via 400 miles of blood vessels. When certain brain areas work hard at something, more blood flows to those regions to help them refuel. The more active your brain, the more energy is consumed. You use energy whenever you use your head, but you certainly don't want to stop thinking.

Managing your energy is like increasing gas mileage in your car. If you run the air conditioner with your windows open, exceed the recommended speed limit, drive all night, and periodically drive with your emergency brake engaged, you are going to consume a lot more gas. So it's essential to tap into your energy sources and prevent those energy drains. And if you can conserve energy as you go along, so much the better.

I want you to think of yourself as a mobile phone. You charge it at night with the expectation that it will be fully charged and ready for you to use by morning. This is the IPE available to you in the morning. It depends on whether or not and how you've changed it. As your day goes by, you use your phone for various things—work, socializing, and the battery begins to deplete. This is productively expended energy, where you are using it productively. Later in the day, you use the same phone with the amount of battery left in it to gossip, scroll social media, play games, read negative news and information, and pass your time. This is unproductive wasted energy. Now, the mobile phone battery is discharged, and you are rushing to charge it may be in the middle of the day. Now charging a phone is easy if you have the charger with you. And this cycle continues. If there is a time when you forget to charge your phone, well, there is no IPE.

Now apply this analogy in your work life. Every day you wake up with a certain amount of IPE your day goes by, you utilize this energy to think creatively, work on your projects, upskill and re-skill yourself, and solve complex work issues. Your energy is getting productively expended. later in the day, you engage in office gossip, fear, overthinking, fearful, hearing negativity, and holding on to grudges. Your energy is getting depleted, and it's UWE here's something interesting. When you engage in unproductive wastage of energy, your battery gets tired at a much faster speed than when you are productively engaging your power.

Winning the leadership game constantly requires a high level of IPE.

## THE PULSE OF PRODUCTIVITY

There's always somewhere to go and something to do—meetings, project deadlines, lunches, presentations, soccer games, doctor appointments. Our energy gets drained out in many ways. But most of us don't stop to consider the importance of energy in our lives until life hits us hard.

Several years ago, I met a senior manager at a mid-size company who aspired to start his consulting venture. He worked at his day job for 12 hours and an additional 3 hours each day to set up his business venture. After nearly two years, he was diagnosed with Meniere's disease, an inner ear disorder. While it's not fatal, he found himself in the unusual position of being tired all the time. His symptoms wore him out, and for most of the days, he felt deprived of his energy. That was the real enemy. He had no desire to chase the once important things to him. He did not think of winning now.

That's the thing about energy; it can drain out of us in so many different ways. Fortunately, there's hope. Lots of hope. We just need to learn how to get our energy back. The fight to reclaim our energy is one of the most important battles we'll ever fight. We're all worn out today in some of the other ways. And you cannot think of winning in this state.

You see, everyone wants to do more—wants to achieve more, wants to get more out of work and life. Everyone wants to be highly productive. We live in a culture that seems to be obsessed with productivity and high performance.

While increasing how much you get done daily is essential, something even more critical rarely gets discussed in the business world. It's energy management.

Here's the big message: No entrepreneur, no leader, and no individual can win over the long run without being fully engaged at their workplace.

Only when people are fully involved in their craft can there be an increase in productivity. One thing every single icon and elite performer I've watched has had in common is the ability to release their most extraordinary productivity. I've always believed that productivity has less to do with time management and more to do with energy management. Energy is the pulse of productivity. Energy is a leader's power. When it's high, you feel like there's no task you can't tackle. When it's low, you feel burnt out and overwhelmed. Implementing an energy-management strategy in your life will help you channel more of your drive toward your work goals.

Don't be an average leader working hard to manage time and agenda so that productivity increases. Be a world-class leader who manages their energy.

Every day there are golden opportunities for us to get back our energy. Here are some random tips to get started. Most of us track time. Today, begin to track your energy. I teach my clients to play the 1–100 game thrice a day. Here are the rules of the game. First, you must be sincere in your efforts. Second, you must play this game alone. And third, you must play the game every day to get the results. So here's how you play the 1–100 game. Every single day when you wake up before you put your foot down on the floor, rate yourself in percentage on a scale of 1–100 (with one being the lowest) on your energy level. Say, for example, you gave yourself a 90% energy level. Now, during lunch, rate your energy level again before sleeping. See if your energy level was consistent at 90, or did it drop low or too low by night. Be conscious of what lowers your energy level. You aim to keep your energy level up throughout the day. There are many ways to keep your energy level up throughout the day. One of the ways I teach my client is to practice energy optimization.

This one practice has changed the lives of more than a million people who I have coached and trained. It's very simple and self-explanatory. The simple technique called EDEG: energy drainers and energy gainers.

Table 9.1 will help you work on your EDEG.

Write down what are things in a day that drain your energy. Think of all the people, projects, situations, and things that drain your energy. It may be something simple as saying a yes when you want to say NO, or maybe it's multitasking that's draining your energy, or perhaps it's too much housework. And then, in the following column, list all the people, projects, situations, and things that help you gain your energy. Maybe working on

**TABLE 9.1**

Energy Gainers and Drainers

| ENERGY DRAINERS | ENERGY GAINERS |
| --- | --- |
| | |
| | |
| | |
| | |

specific projects energizes you. Or it might be certain people you meet or talk with who energize you.

Take a good look at both lists. And begin to maximize your energy gainers. While you cannot avoid working with the energy drainers, you must learn to maximize and leverage your energy gainers.

---

## PERSONAL ENERGY BECOMES COMPANY ENERGY

Émilie du Châtelet said that energy could neither be created nor destroyed; it can only be transformed or transferred from one form to another. This means the level of energy you bring to your workplace can be transferred to your teams and can be passed on to your projects to work that you do. I wish I had known this principle early on in my life.

From an energy perspective, it's not surprising that your journey as a leader can feel like an emotional roller coaster. You go from happy to sad, content to hungry, in control, and overwhelmed in your journey. When you interact with others, you sense and respond to their energies, the same as they respond to yours. We do not usually talk about this unseen, subtle communication, but everyone does it.

In my own career, I realized that there were times that I wasn't a happy boss/leader for my employees to follow. You are the person that everyone feeds from, and my emotions affect everyone around me. If I were going through a rough time, then employees and the client and management would be too, by extension.

I soon learned that personal energy becomes company energy.

Each person's energy creates the environment at your work; anyone who associates with the company brings in the energy—from the janitor to your clients to your CEO, everyone is responsible for the energy created at the organization. Everyone feeds off everyone's energy like a chain reaction. We absorb each other's energy. Think of the times when you woke up feeling fresh, wanting to seize the day. You are happy and are moving from one meeting to another in high spirits. By noon you get an email from a client about how rough the times are for him and that he would need to discontinue the contract with your company. This gets you in an off mood, and in the following potential client meeting you have, you are anxious and not too in high spirits. That impacts your sales potential. You feel frustrated with yourself, and at that time, your assistant walks in to talk with you about an upcoming talk you have to deliver next week. You speak with her rather rudely because of your mood. She takes the brunt, and when she is at her desk, a team member emails her for some clarification, to whom she responds curtly. That team member is now off mood with this behavior and passes that to whomever he deals with in the organization, including the clients. And the chain continues.

You see how one person's low energy level impacts the entire organization. Similarly, one person's high energy level affects the rest of the organization. This is why every person in the organization must be energy-sensitive. And it starts with you.

Our whole Planet Earth is composed of an infinite reservoir of energy, as is the human body, and it's inevitable to get in contact with other people's power. Scientists now know that human beings and everything else in our world is composed of specifically arranged amalgamations of vibrating electrical energy that we perceive as physicality. We are composed entirely of energy, regardless of whether we can see or feel it.

How is this related to winning? When you find yourself in situations that trigger your insecurities, others can sense your fear. Because of the nature of the human ego, some will even prey upon the weakness they perceive in you, which further dissolves your confidence.

So how do you stop absorbing other people's negative energy? How can you dispel negative energy? How can you perform your best by keeping your energy at high levels?

## CHANGE THE MEANING, CHANGE YOUR ENERGY

Energy, not time, is the fundamental currency of high performance. If we want to perform at our best, we must first and foremost manage our energy, not our time. If you're going to break the chain of absorbing other people's negative energy and letting it impact you, is a technique called M3. Later, this technique I derived was featured in People Matters, a well-known Human Resources Magazine.

M3 stands for Meaning Making Machine. On a particular day, three men were working in one place. Another man came by and asked the first man, 'What are you doing here?' The man looked up and said, 'Are you blind? Can't you see I'm cutting stone?' This person moved on to the next man and asked, 'What are *you* doing here?' That man looked up and said, 'Something to fill my belly. So I come here and do whatever they ask me to do. I just have to fill my belly, that's all.' He went to the third man and asked, 'What are *you* doing here?' That man stood up in great joy and said, 'I'm building a beautiful temple here!' All of them were doing the same thing, but the meaning of what they were doing was different. What meaning are you giving to your work, situations, relationships, and interactions with people?

As humans, we interpret everything that happens to us and with us. You can look at any of your situations and create your very own narrative inside your head. Most of the things that happen to you are because of the meaning you give it. If you have a boss who looks stern and rarely smiles, what meaning do you put? Do you say that he is rude or a micromanager, or do you say that he must be merely busy and caught up with work? The meaning you will give will decide your energy level and your course of action toward your boss. If you say to yourself that your boss is rude, you will constantly end negative energy to him and probably distance yourself from him, you will hesitate to share your ideas with him, and your slightest interaction with him will cause friction. You will generate stress in your life. And if you say to yourself that he might be caught up with work, you will find positive energy in yourself, and your actions will be in ways that help to connect with him and know his problem and help with solutions. You will generate a pathway of success for yourself.

Has it ever happened with you that while walking toward the cafeteria, you waved at your colleague, but she did not respond? Do you give it the meaning that she is mad at you, or do you say that she simply must not have seen you? In 30 seconds, you can move from success to stress or stress to success by merely giving meaning. Because whatever meaning you provide will determine your response, and your response will finally determine the level of your growth and success. Your interpretation of things is always the cause of your actions. Here's what happens in 30 seconds:

1. Something external happens, an event—perhaps a passing comment from a colleague.
2. You assess the event and put a meaning to it.
3. As a result of the meaning, you generate an emotion such as fear, hope, joy, anger, or guilt.
4. The emotions trigger an action that leads to your result.

All of the above take place in 30 seconds. You see, stress is self-created. Outside situations and people can never be the cause of your stress. Stress is generated from within by the meaning you put into everything around you. Nothing in the world means anything until you decide what meaning to give it.

The problem is that we humans are wired to give negative meaning to everything we face. Some of us have done a triple Ph.D. in giving negative connotations to situations. We need to recognize this 'meaning-making' process and the subsequent stories we invent. Instead, try to see the event for what occurred without adding 'color.' Gather relevant information and evidence.

In circumstances of any kind, if you feel jealousy, fear authority, or hold other critical or judgmental thoughts about others, your confidence shakes. These things happen purely because of our meaning to people's behaviors and circumstances.

External situations cause not all energy levels. Most of it is because of our thinking and overthinking. Your thoughts, not the world, cause your stress. You can change your views of stress at any given moment and eliminate the anxiety for the next few moments or even hours and days simply by practicing M3.

Change the meaning and change your energy which will change your actions. Make a conscious choice to select a meaning that will activate high energy. Every meaning you give to situations or people has an energy that will strengthen or weaken you.

Knowing that you can choose what something means to you can give you great power and a sense of security that you never had. So *give the meaning that will change everything in your favor and open the pathway to your leadership success.*

## ENERGY RITUALS FOR RENEWAL

Our work culture belief is that 'more is better.' Our work culture teaches us to be constantly busy. Busy is better is what we hear. If you aren't busy, you are looked down upon.

Almost every time I ask someone how things are going? I get this answer: Oh, I am so busy! We seem so proud to let someone know that we are busy. We live in a society that glorifies busyness. We think a super busy person might be of higher status—that being busy = more money, more business, more success. Not being busy has become Taboo in our society. Working hard is admirable or doubtful. But busyness is not equal to business; it's not equal to being productive.

I want you to think about the vibration the word busy releases deeply? It says I am stressed; I am not available for you. I do not have time for myself. It sends a strong message that I don't have time for anyone and anything. And this manifests into reality in our work environment. That's why we see everyone around us working in tension and anxiety. Check the number of times you have said—I don't have time, or it's so hard to find the time. We've got a habit to repeatedly say 'I am busy.'

The word 'busy' itself is an energy drainer.

These days, most professionals work longer hours, attend more meetings, take shorter vacations, answer more emails, and eat lunch at their desks; if you eat lunch at all! The way we're working isn't working. Demand is exceeding our capacity. Today it's all about 'more, bigger, faster,' undermining our energy, focus, creativity, and passion. Nearly 75% of employees worldwide feel disengaged at work every day. And it's all affecting the bottom line. The real issue is not the number of hours we sit behind the desk but the energy we bring to our work and the value we generate.

Do you want to perform at a higher level? Take care of your IPE. There are many ways to renew your IPE. Some renewing activities are going for a walk, having a conversation with a work buddy, doing a quick workout, meditating, doing some breathing exercises, taking a nap, or whatever. All of these renew your energy and optimize your performance for the subsequent 90–120 minute work or complete performance section. Now here's the key with those energy-renewing activities. You want to turn them into rituals.

Here's a 3-D way to increase productivity by conserving your energy. All you need to do is answer these three questions every single day:

1. What can I do?
2. What can I delete?
3. What can I delegate?

The more you are clear on the above three questions, the more you will conserve your energy. Once you make this a ritual, you will have time for meditating, walking, resting, and reflecting, all of which will help conserve and renew the IPE.

We all have a sense of our energy level, whether we feel productive or not, whether we're alert and excited or tired and groggy, but most of us try to ignore its underlying effect on our work.

Money is not the great currency of our time. Energy is—physical energy to get out of bed and positive energy to do something better with our lives. Your intention to win the leadership game means nothing if you don't have the power to win.

---

## RAPID ACTION PLAN

Write one action you will do today to optimize your energy levels.

# Conclusion: The Winner Takes It All

It's the final moment before an important presentation. The stage was lit up. It was every speaker's dream. The auditorium was filled with 25,000 people who had come to the widely popular leadership summit in Atlanta from America and Canada. It was my very first public appearance in the 11 years of my leadership speaking career. Up until now, I was only speaking in corporate training rooms. But this time, it was a huge public event. I had prepared for this day, not since a week, not since a month, not even for six months. I had prepared for this day for the past nine and a half years. I had always dreamt of being a part of a massive event like this, where I would share the stage along with some of the best industry speakers from America. Up until now, I felt good and confident. But as I heard my name being announced, suddenly something shifted in me. I felt a wave of self-doubt. I started questioning my preparation. The urge to run away and sabotage the whole thing started bubbling to the surface. As hard as you try to overcome your inexplicable insecurity, something tells you that you've already lost.

I lost that day on stage. Fear overtook all of my preparation and self-doubt killed my success. I stammered while spoke. I wasn't clear and confident in my message. I played small. I failed. And when you fail, it hurts real bad. You feel as if your soul has been ripped apart. That moment I knew that no one would ever call me on stage again and that women of Indian-descents would always be seen as someone who can work heads down in an office.

For the next few months, my life and work was dragging. I lost all hope of becoming iconic in the field of leadership. And in this gloominess of my mood, while driving my younger daughter to soccer practice, I read a sign-board on the sidewalk that read, 'nothing changes until you change.'

DOI: 10.4324/9781003260714-12

And that's when it struck me that I was doing the hard work, I was preparing more than anyone else, I was upskilling myself, but yet I was failing on a large magnitude. And the reason was that I wasn't working inside of myself.

The beauty of leadership? It doesn't depend on external situations. Leadership is an inside game and it can never be won externally until it's mastered internally. And I was playing the game wrong. I was playing it externally without mastering it internally. I lost internally the battle of self-doubt and fear because of which I failed externally.

Yes, my friend, winning or losing begins in your mind. Whether you will win on the day of your game depends if you've been practicing to win daily in your mind. In your day-to-day situation, do you win the battle of the mind? Winning is defined as something you win. And the most significant thing you can ever win over is your mind. Conquer this territory, and you will win every game.

And let me tell you something, it's a battlefield within you. Your mind is a battlefield, and the battle of our life is always won or lost in your mind. Every day you are engaged in a battle of which you are unaware. Have you ever wondered why you lose your temper? Why do you find it challenging to give up on some habits? Why do you behave the way you do?

It's because constantly, there is a war in your mind. We ignore this war, the war of our thoughts. Our thoughts seem to be playing automatically on us. And so we act. I wish performance evaluations were based on the employee's thought processes rather than their actions.

I wish we could focus more on transforming employees rather than only training them because transformation occurs inside you. And when you are changed for the better, you begin winning. And in this war, your opponent is not your boss or your team or your spouse or your friends. It's you. Most of us ignore the battle of our minds and remain average players in the game.

Nothing will hinder your progress or help you move ahead in life as much as your mind. When I use the word mind, I refer to the system of thoughts, the way of thinking in which a person approaches life. Our lives are always moving in the direction of the most dominant thought. Today when you look into the mirror, the person who stares back, that person has been shaped with your thoughts of yesterday and will be shaped by your thoughts of today. What you think is what you become.

As proverb 23: 7 reads, 'For as he thinketh in the heart, so is he.' To win the game outside, you've got to win the game inside. And the war of the mind is the war of thoughts. Each human being on this planet earth has been given the power of ideas to win or lose the game one plays. You need to ask yourself now, do I like the direction my thoughts are taking me? If your answer is no, then it's time to change your thoughts.

*I will tell you a story my father once said to me as a kid, whose father as a horse trainer was moving from stable to stable, from ranch to ranch, training horses. Thus, the boy's school career was constantly interrupted. When he was a senior, the teacher asked him to write about what he wanted to be when he grew up. He did not hesitate a minute and wrote a seven-page paper about his aim to be an owner of a horse ranch; he wrote many details and drew a location of buildings and stables and even a detailed house plan.*

*He received his paperback with the letter 'F' on the front page two days later. After class, he came to the teacher and asked: 'Why did I receive an F?'. The teacher responded: 'This dream is so unrealistic for a boy like you, who has no money, no resources and who comes from an illiterate family. There is no possibility that you will reach your great goals one day.' Then the teacher offered to rewrite the paper with a more realistic attitude.*

*The boy went home and asked his father how he should act. The father answered: 'This decision is crucial for you. So you have to make your mind about this.'*

*After several days, the boy brought the same paper to his teacher. No changes were made. He said: 'Keep the F, and I will keep my dream.'*

*Today this bow has grown up to own a 4,000-square-foot house in the middle of a 200-acre horse ranch, and he still has that school paper, which now is framed over the fireplace.*

Remember, you have to follow your heart, never give up, move on with determination and persistence, and never let anyone take your dreams away.

My friend, the real battle is taking place in your mind. If you're defeated in your thoughts, you've already lost. Your career life will be full of hardships and opportunities. All your thoughts combine to make your actions that will decide if you win or lose. You can either have doubt or faith in your mind. But you can't have both.

The longer I live, and the more I coach executives to win their game, the more I realize that winning is from the inside. Winning from the inside is about how you feel about yourself. There are always two games in your life: the inner game and the outer game. If you ignore your inner game, you never play your best in the external game. One of the essential elements of winning the external leadership game is overcoming the internal obstacles we create like self-doubt, anxiety, tension, worry, self-sabotaging, jealousy, anger, hatred, limiting beliefs.

My father would often say that you can take the horse to the water, but you can't force it to drink the water. In my 21 years of coaching people, I've helped numerous professionals to cross the deep chasm between where they are and where they want to be. And those who have crossed the abyss are the ones who had the desire internally to do so.

Whether we realize it or not, we often internally talk to ourselves. We give ourselves instructions. I have a confession to make. Though my books are now bestsellers, though I speak at corporations and events worldwide, though I am known for redefining leadership, there are many battles I lost in my life only because of my limiting internal talk.

I am not alone. Millions of people play small in their lives simply because of their disempowering internal talk. When most people are performing a task, there's a conversation going on in their heads. I began to separate myself into two beings. I always see a small Payal inside the big Payal. The small me is full of doubts and stops the big Payal from playing big. This small me is usually obsessed with the should and shouldn't and is always trying to tell me that the road ahead could be dangerous. I then send my big me to talk to it. The significant me is prosperous and influential and isn't afraid to play big. The big me is constantly empowering the small me, and soon the tiny me is quite allowing the big me to win. What has your internal talk been like?

Shake off the doubt. Shake off the negative voices. The universe wouldn't have put that dream in your heart if it wasn't already planning on bringing it to pass, and you don't have to figure out how it's going to happen. It may not work on paper. The odds may be against you. That's okay; that's not your job. Your job is to fill your minds with belief. I always believe that one must walk by faith, not by sight. The scripture says the things we see are only temporary, but what we hear, deep inside of us, that's permanent.

To win the leadership game, you must keep reprograming and conditioning your minds for success.

The most challenging game you will ever play is the game inside of your mind. Your inner game will make you or break you. Every day you will notice there is a terrible fight inside of you. The small you is full of anger, envy, sorrow, regret, greed, arrogance, self-pity, guilt, resentment, inferiority, lies, false pride, superiority, doubt, and ego. The other is the big you full of joy, peace, love, hope, serenity, humility, kindness, benevolence, empathy, generosity, truth, compassion, and faith. Every day you must make the big win.

In my early career years, one of my mentors once told me that inside each of us are two wolves, and the one that wins is the one you feed most. Who do you provide most—the big you or the small you.

Win over self-doubt, your fears, your worry, over the opinions of people, over hatred. Win over the lies you tell yourself about yourself that you aren't good enough. Set yourself up to win by celebrating your micro successes. Every day there are micro wins in our life. When you see your micro wins, consciously remind yourself that you are winning the battle of your mind.

No one knows what you went through to get there. No one understands what you'll have to do again to get there. Winning is an addiction. Winning is craziness. Winning requires real talk. Every day is a new challenge, both internal and external. Who told you that you couldn't be successful? Who told you, you could only get here? Who told you are not smart enough, that you've reached your limits? I can assure you that it did not come from inside of you. You did not create these thoughts for yourself. Those are all coming from the people and the information you read. Don't let what anyone told you or showed you limit your life. Start reprograming your mind. All through the day, dwell on the truth that you are created to win, that you are blessed, healthy, talented, and valuable.

You are the one who is going to create the life that you want. You're going to keep that winning spirit in the difficult times. It's you my friend who is responsible for the game you are playing. The game is long. The game is tough. The game is always changing. New players will join in. Competition will be killing. And I encourage you to grow through it all and finish strong.

And know this my friend, the game isn't over until you win. Because in the end, the winner takes it all.

# Index

*Note*: Page numbers in **bold** refer to tables and those in *italic* refer to figures.

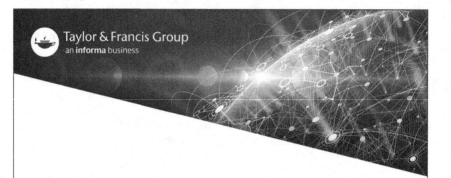

Printed in the United States
by Baker & Taylor Publisher Services

Printed in the United States
by Baker & Taylor Publisher Services